ARBITRARY BORDERS
Political Boundaries in World History

The Division of the Middle East
The Treaty of Sèvres

Northern Ireland and England
The Troubles

The Great Wall of China

The Green Line
The Division of Palestine

The Iron Curtain
The Cold War in Europe

The Mason–Dixon Line

Vietnam: The 17th Parallel

Korea: The 38th Parallel and the Demilitarized Zone

The U.S.–Mexico Border
The Treaty of Guadalupe Hidalgo

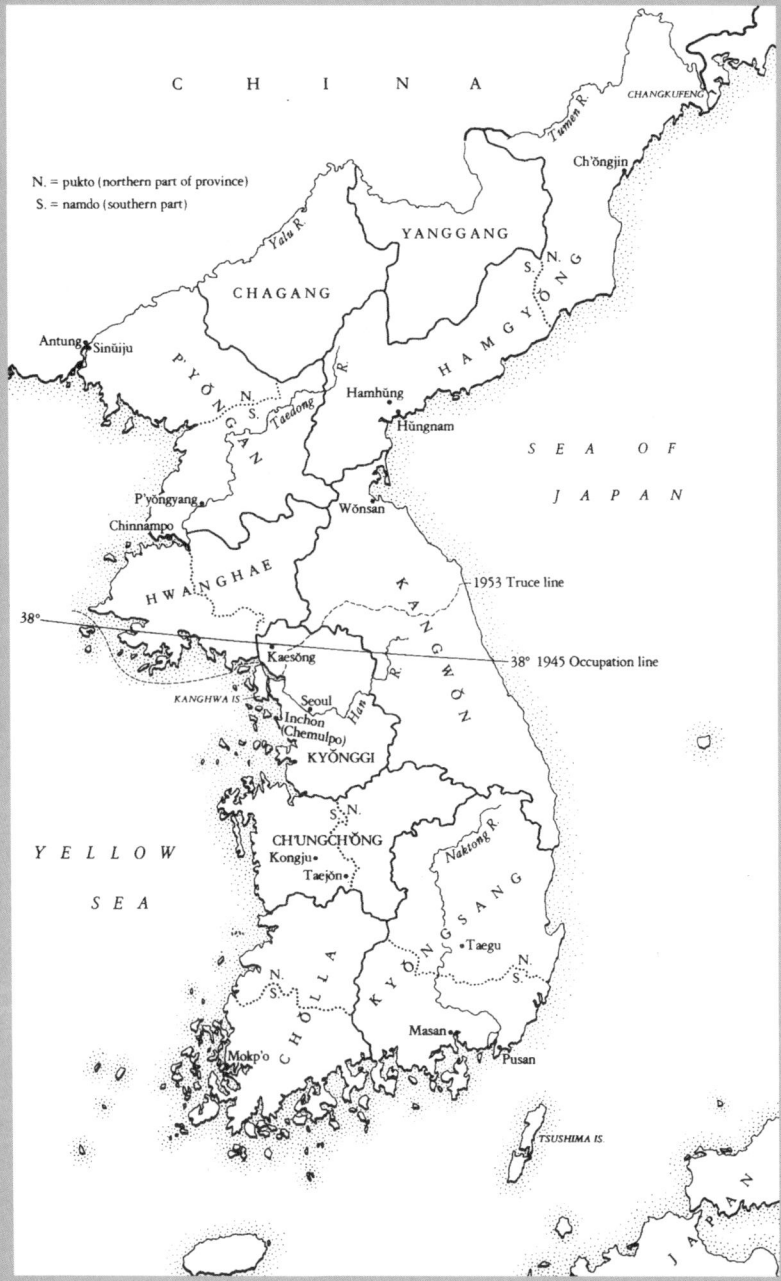

Korea in recent times.

ARBITRARY BORDERS

Political Boundaries in World History

Korea Divided
The 38th Parallel and the Demilitarized Zone

James I. Matray

Foreword by
Senator **George J. Mitchell**

Introduction by
James I. Matray
California State University, Chico

Mishawaka-Penn-Harris
Public Library
Mishawaka, Indiana

Philadelphia

FRONTIS Map of Korea, divided into northern and southern sections at the 38th Parallel.

CHELSEA HOUSE PUBLISHERS

VP, NEW PRODUCT DEVELOPMENT Sally Cheney
DIRECTOR OF PRODUCTION Kim Shinners
CREATIVE MANAGER Takeshi Takahashi
MANUFACTURING MANAGER Diann Grasse

Staff for KOREA DIVIDED

EXECUTIVE EDITOR Lee Marcott
PRODUCTION EDITOR Noelle Nardone
ASSOCIATE PHOTO EDITOR Noelle Nardone
SERIES DESIGNER Keith Trego
COVER DESIGNER Keith Trego
LAYOUT EJB Publishing Services

©2005 by Chelsea House Publishers,
a subsidiary of Haights Cross Communications.
All rights reserved. Printed and bound in the United States of America.

A Haights Cross Communications Company

www.chelseahouse.com

First Printing

9 8 7 6 5 4 3 2 1

Library of Congress Cataloging-in-Publication Data
Matray, James Irving, 1948-
  Korea divided : the thirty-eighth parallel and the Demilitarized Zone / by James I. Matray.
     p. cm. — (Arbitrary borders)
  Audience: Grades 9-12.
  Includes bibliographical references.
  ISBN 0-7910-7829-9
  1. Korea—History—Juvenile literature. I. Title: Thirty-eighth parallel and the Demilitarized Zone. II. Title: 38th parallel and the Demilitarized Zone. III. Title. IV. Series.
  DS907.4.M37 2004
  951.904—dc22
                              2004009771

All links and web addresses were checked and verified to be correct at the time of publication. Because of the dynamic nature of the web, some addresses and links may have changed since publication and may no longer be valid.

*To My History Family
at Chico State*

Contents

	Foreword by Senator George J. Mitchell	viii
	Introduction by James I. Matray	xi
	Map	xiii
	List of Abbreviations	xiv
1	Just One Korea	1
2	Early Artificial Borders	15
3	Imperialist Impositions	30
4	Drawing the Line	44
5	A House Divided	57
6	Koreans Invade Korea	71
7	Partition for Peace	85
8	South of the Border	100
9	North of the Border	114
10	Wish and Reality	128
	Chronology and Timeline	142
	Notes	147
	Bibliography	151
	Index	155

Foreword

Senator George J. Mitchell

I spent years working for peace in Northern Ireland and in the Middle East. I also made many visits to the Balkans during the long and violent conflict there.

Each of the three areas is unique; so is each conflict. But there are also some similarities: in each, there are differences over religion, national identity, and territory.

Deep religious differences that lead to murderous hostility are common in human history. Competing aspirations involving national identity are more recent occurrences, but often have been just as deadly.

Territorial disputes—two or more people claiming the same land—are as old as humankind. Almost without exception, such disputes have been a factor in recent conflicts. It is impossible to calculate the extent to which the demand for land—as opposed to religion, national identity, or other factors—figures in the motivation of people caught up in conflict. In my experience it is a substantial factor that has played a role in each of the three conflicts mentioned above.

In Northern Ireland and the Middle East, the location of the border was a major factor in igniting and sustaining the conflict. And it is memorialized in a dramatic and visible way: through the construction of large walls whose purpose is to physically separate the two communities.

In Belfast, the capital and largest city in Northern Ireland, the so-called "Peace Line" cuts through the heart of the city, right across urban streets. Up to thirty feet high in places, topped with barbed wire in others, it is an ugly reminder of the duration and intensity of the conflict.

In the Middle East, as I write these words, the government of Israel has embarked on a huge and controversial effort to construct a security fence roughly along the line that separates Israel from the West Bank.

Having served a tour of duty with the U.S. Army in Berlin, which was once the site of the best known of modern walls, I am skeptical of their long-term value, although they often serve short-term needs. But it cannot be said that such structures represent a new idea. Ancient China built the Great Wall to deter nomadic Mongol tribes from attacking its population.

In much the same way, other early societies established boundaries and fortified them militarily to achieve the goal of self-protection. Borders always have separated people. Indeed, that is their purpose.

This series of books examines the important and timely issue of the significance of arbitrary borders in history. Each volume focuses attention on a territorial division, but the analytical approach is more comprehensive. These studies describe arbitrary borders as places where people interact differently from the way they would if the boundary did not exist. This pattern is especially pronounced where there is no geographic reason for the boundary and no history recognizing its legitimacy. Even though many borders have been defined without legal precision, governments frequently have provided vigorous monitoring and military defense for them.

This series will show how the migration of people and exchange of goods almost always work to undermine the separation that borders seek to maintain. The continuing evolution of a European community provides a contemporary example illustrating this point, most obviously with the adoption of a single currency. Moreover, even former Soviet bloc nations have eliminated barriers to economic and political integration.

Globalization has emerged as one of the most powerful forces in international affairs during the twenty-first century. Not only have markets for the exchange of goods and services become genuinely worldwide, but instant communication and sharing of information have shattered old barriers separating people. Some scholars even argue that globalization has made the entire concept of a territorial nation-state irrelevant. Although the assertion is certainly premature and probably wrong, it highlights the importance of recognizing how borders often have reflected and affirmed the cultural, ethnic, or linguistic perimeters that define a people or a country.

Since the Cold War ended, competition over resources or a variety of interests threaten boundaries more than ever, resulting in contentious interaction, conflict, adaptation, and intermixture. How people define their borders is also a factor in determining how events develop in the surrounding region. This series will provide detailed descriptions of selected arbitrary borders in history with the objective of providing insights on how artificial boundaries separating people will influence international affairs during the next century.

Senator George J. Mitchell
October 2003

Introduction

James I. Matray
California State University, Chico

Throughout history, borders have separated people. Scholars have devoted considerable attention to assessing the significance and impact of territorial boundaries on the course of human history, explaining how they often have been sources of controversy and conflict. In the modern age, the rise of nation-states in Europe created the need for governments to negotiate treaties to confirm boundary lines that periodically changed as a consequence of wars and revolutions. European expansion in the nineteenth century imposed new borders on Africa and Asia. Many native peoples viewed these boundaries as arbitrary and, after independence, continued to contest their legitimacy. At the end of both world wars in the twentieth century, world leaders drew artificial and impermanent lines separating assorted people around the globe. Borders certainly are among the most important factors that have influenced the development of world affairs.

Chelsea House Publishers decided to publish a collection of books looking at arbitrary borders in history in response to the revival of the nuclear crisis in North Korea in October 2002. Recent tensions on the Korean peninsula are a direct consequence of Korea's partition at the 38th parallel at the end of World War II. Other nations in human history have suffered because of similar artificial divisions that have been the result of either international or domestic factors and often a combination of both. In the case of Korea, the United States and the Soviet Union decided in August 1945 to divide the country into two zones of military occupation ostensibly to facilitate the surrender of Japanese forces. However, a political contest was then underway inside Korea to determine the future of the nation after forty years of Japanese colonial rule. The Cold War then created two Koreas with sharply contrasting political, social, and economic systems that symbolized an ideological split among the Korean people. Borders separate people, but rarely prevent their economic, political, social, and cultural interaction. But in Korea, an artificial border has existed since 1945 as a nearly impenetrable barrier precluding meaningful contact between two portions of the same population. Ultimately, two authentic Koreas emerged, exposing how an arbitrary boundary can create circumstances resulting even in the permanent division of a homogeneous people in a historically united land.

Korea's experience in dealing with artificial division may well be unique, but it is not without historical parallels. The first set of books in this series on arbitrary boundaries will provide description and analysis of the division of the Middle East after World War I, the Iron Curtain in Central Europe during the Cold War, the United States-Mexico border, the 17th parallel in Vietnam, and the Mason-Dixon Line. A second set of books will address the Great Wall in China, the Green Line in Israel, and the 38th parallel and demilitarized zone in Korea. Finally, there will be volumes describing how discord over artificial borders in the Louisiana Territory, Northern Ireland, and Czechoslovakia reflected fundamental disputes about sovereignty, religion, and ethnicity. Admittedly, there are many significant differences between these boundaries, but these books will strive to cover as many common themes as possible. In so doing, each will help readers conceptualize how complex factors such as colonialism, culture, and economics determine the nature of contact between people along these borders. Although globalization has emerged as a powerful force working against the creation and maintenance of lines separating people, boundaries likely will endure as factors having a persistent influence on world events. This series of books will provide insights about the impact of arbitrary borders on human history and how such borders continue to shape the modern world.

James I. Matray
Chico, California
April 2004

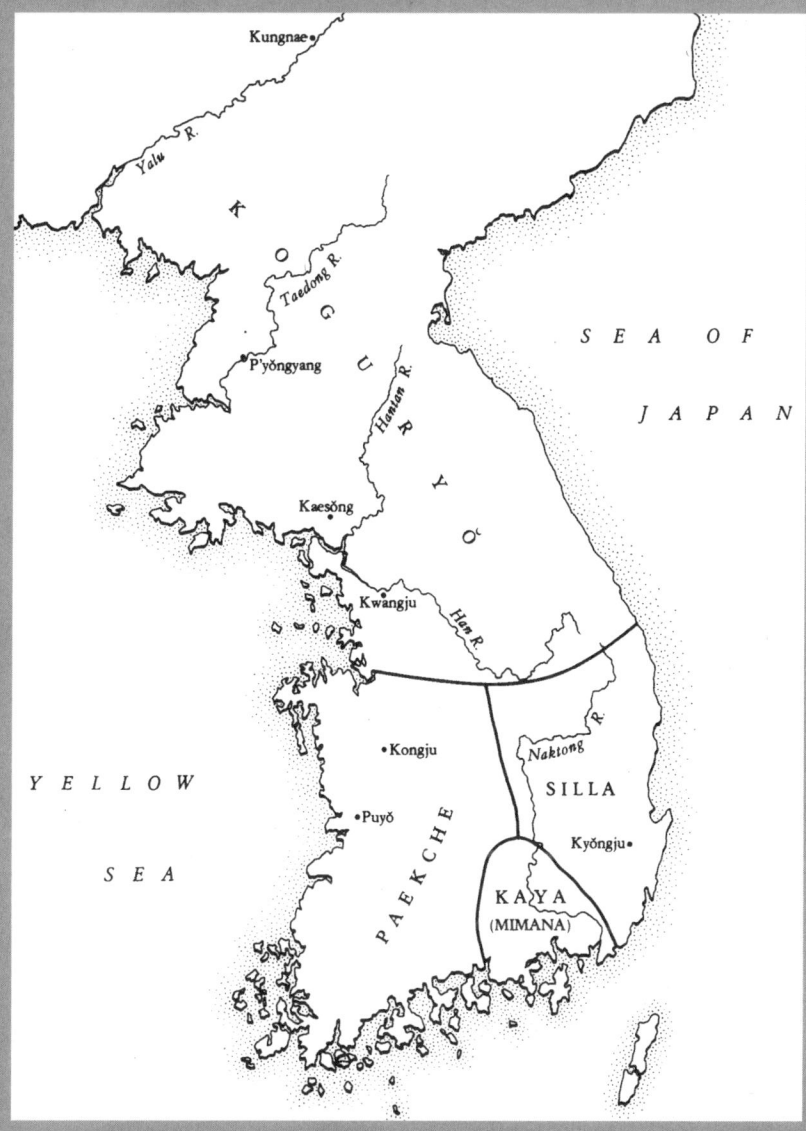

Korea during the Three Kingdoms Period (around 500 A.D.)

LIST OF ABBREVIATIONS

DFUF:	Democratic Front for the Unification of the Fatherland
DMZ:	demilitarized zone
DPRK:	Democratic People's Republic of Korea
IAEA:	International Atomic Energy Agency
JCS:	Joint Chiefs of Staff
KCIA:	Korean Central Intelligence Agency
KPA:	Korean People's Army
KPG:	Korean Provisional Government
KPR:	Korean People's Republic
KWP:	Korean Workers' Party
MAC:	Military Armistice Commission
NPT:	Nuclear Non-Proliferation Treaty
POW:	prisoner of war
PRC:	People's Republic of China
ROK:	Republic of Korea
SKIG:	South Korean Interim Government
SKILA:	South Korean Interim Legislative Assembly
UN:	United Nations
UNC:	United Nations Command
UNKRA:	United Nations Korean Reconstruction Agency
UNTCOK:	United Nations Temporary Commission on Korea

1

Just One Korea

April 1948 held a moment of great tension in the history of Korea. That month, Kim Kyu-sik, a revered patriot and nationalist leader, traveled to the northern city of Pyongyang in a desperate attempt to prevent the creation of two Koreas. At the age of 67, his reputation for integrity and selflessness together with his political skill and tireless dedication gave reason for optimism that a North-South Conference would eliminate the arbitrary boundary dividing the nation. In August 1945, the Soviet Union had accepted an eleventh-hour U.S. proposal for division of the Korean peninsula at the thirty-eighth parallel into two zones of military occupation. Koreans without exception rejected the legitimacy of this artificial border. At the North-South Conference in 1948, Kim Kyu-sik failed to find a way to block formation of two governments in Korea, each of which claimed to control the entire country. During 1949, the determination of the Republic of Korea (ROK) in the south and the Democratic People's Republic of Korea (DPRK) in the north to reunite the peninsula led to violent border clashes along the parallel. The conventional phase of the Korean War began in June 1950 when North Korea attacked South Korea. Historian Bruce Cumings emphasized the importance of remembering that there was just one Korea when he noted "the ultimate irony" of the words "Koreans invade Korea."[1] In July 1953, as a result of an armistice, a demilitarized zone (DMZ) was substituted for the thirty-eighth parallel as the marker that partitioned Korea. Despite the end of the Cold War in 1989, this arbitrary border still separated the two Koreas at the beginning of the twenty-first century.

Korean leaders recognized immediately after World War II that the thirty-eighth parallel might become a permanent line dividing the peninsula. Their fears grew early in 1948 when the United Nations, after creation of a United Nations Temporary Commission on Korea (UNTCOK) under the resolution of November 14, 1947, authorized elections only in southern Korea for representatives in a legislative assembly. Kim Kyu-sik, chair of the South Korean Interim Legislative Assembly (SKILA), and

Kim Gu, leader of the Korean Independence Party, opposed separate elections, predicting that this would make Korea's division permanent. Other moderate and left-wing politicians insisted that an agreement was still possible with the North Korean government. Eager to maximize popular participation, Lieutenant General John R. Hodge, the U.S. occupation commander, invited both Kims and conservative politician Syngman Rhee to a meeting to solicit support for elections in the south alone. Kim Kyu-sik stated that he and Kim Gu "agree that an election for South Korea would be postponed until we can hold a joint conference with the leaders of the North." Two hours of conversation failed to change his mind. On February 21, Kim Gu announced at a press conference that he opposed separate elections. Later, U.S. embassy official Gregory Henderson observed that temporary division created a political opening for others: "Rhee, deft in footwork, at first privately indicated acceptance, then ducked out leaving the others exposed and holding the bag."[2] For him, half a loaf would be enough.

In December 1947, Cho So-ang, president of the National Congress, Yo Un-hong, chief of the Socialist Democratic Party and brother of famous patriot Yo Un-hyong (who had been assassinated that year), and the two Kims had begun to discuss ways for Koreans themselves to remove Korea's artificial border. At a meeting of 12 parties, there was agreement that neither a conference of the major powers nor the United Nations (UN) could agree on a reunification plan so long as the Cold War continued to generate international tensions. Kim Kyu-sik warned that if the Communists or the North Koreans proposed the conference, "the extreme rightists might try to oppose it; but if the suggestion should first come from the [UNTCOK], it might have greater weight." He stressed, however, that prior to a North-South Conference, the occupation commanders in both zones had to free political prisoners; cancel or suspend warrants for the arrest of Korean political leaders; respect freedom of speech, press, assembly, and association; and announce details for withdrawal of all occupation forces.[3]

On March 12, 1948, Kim Kyu-sik, Kim Gu, Cho So-ang, and Hong Myong-hui, leader of the Democratic Independence Party, issued a joint statement pledging to work for unified Korean independence and vowing not to participate in a separate election, which would be the equivalent of committing "murder in a family." In a letter to Kim Il Sung, chair of the North Korean People's Committee, and Kim Du-bong, head of the North Korean Workers Party, they proposed, "measures for establishment of a unified and democratic government should be discussed through a conference of political leaders of North and South."[4] Kim Kyu-sik met with members of the UNTCOK to

> **UN RESOLUTION OF NOVEMBER 14, 1947**
>
> The UN resolution of November 14, 1947, provided a plan for peaceful removal of the arbitrary boundary that divided Korea after World War II. It also marked the beginning of UN involvement in the Soviet-American dispute over Korea's postwar future and created the foundation for its decision to intervene militarily in the Korean War. In August 1947, the Truman administration, in response to failure of the Joint Soviet-American Commission to devise a plan to reunify Korea, approved a policy paper outlining various methods of ending the deadlock. If the Soviet Union was uncooperative, the U.S. plan provided for referral of the Korean issue to the UN. On September 4, Moscow rejected Washington's proposal for a four-power conference to discuss steps toward achieving Korea's unity and economic recovery, resulting in the United States' resorting to the international organization.
>
> Less than two weeks later, Secretary of State George C. Marshall delivered a speech to the UN General Assembly and placed the Korean matter on its agenda. The State Department already had in hand a draft resolution calling for UN-supervised free elections for delegates to a national assembly within six months of adoption. This legislature, reflecting the two-to-one population superiority of southern Korea, would formulate a constitution and appoint officials to serve in a provisional government. Perhaps the most important provision outlined for the creation of a UN Temporary Commission on Korea (UNTCOK), comprising 11 nations, to supervise the elections, foster freedom of choice, and report findings to the General Assembly.

dissuade them from agreeing to observe and then certify the election, because

> any Korean who talked about a South Korean unilateral government will go down in history as a "bad egg" because once that term is used, the Communists in the North under the direction of the Soviet Union will establish what is called a "People's Republic." ... Then you will have two unilateral governments in this little space of something over 85,000 square miles. Not only that, but once such a thing occurs in history, it will go down forever, and it will be perpetuated; then you are

---

Warren R. Austin, in his capacity as U.S. permanent representative, presented a revised draft resolution on October 17 calling for elections no later than March 31, 1948, and incorporating Moscow's proposal for Soviet-American military withdrawal 90 days after the formation of a provisional government. On November 14, the UN General Assembly passed the U.S.-sponsored resolution by a wide margin. Nine nations were to serve on the UNTCOK: Canada, the Republic of China, Australia, France, El Salvador, the Philippines, Syria, India, and Ukraine. Some members of the UNTCOK voiced misgivings about becoming involved in the dispute over Korea, especially after Ukraine refused to participate. When the commission arrived in Korea, the Soviet occupation commander denied access to the north, causing the United States to urge the UNTCOK to supervise elections only in the U.S. zone. Bowing to U.S. pressure, the UN sanctioned an election confined to southern Korea.

On May 10, 1948, the UNTCOK observed balloting for the selection of national assembly delegates, leading to formation of the ROK the following August. The UNTCOK's judgment that the election results reflected the freely expressed will of the people gave the ROK an international stamp of legitimacy. UN involvement in creating the ROK established a moral commitment that would result in passage of the UN Security Council resolutions of June 25 and June 27, 1950, calling on member nations to come to the assistance of the ROK after the North Korean invasion of South Korea.

In April 1948, Korean leaders met in hopes of preventing the division of Korea, but the artificial boundaries established during World War II proved too strong to break. Shown here is the Japanese-constructed Capitol Building in Seoul, the current capital of South Korea, during a 1948 rally. The ROK government demolished the structure in 1997 to eliminate a constant reminder of colonial rule.

responsible and we are responsible for perpetuating the division of Korea into a Northern half and a Southern half.[5]

Despite Kim's efforts, a majority of the UNTCOK voted to observe the elections, scheduled for May 10, 1948, only in the American occupation zone.

On March 25, Radio Pyongyang broadcast an invitation to all South Korean parties, associations, and organizations that opposed elections separate from those of the Central Committee of the Democratic National Coalition Front to meet on April 14 in Pyongyang with the representatives of North Korean political parties and social organizations. Kim Il Sung also sent a formal letter to Kim Kyu-sik officially inviting 15 South Korean conservative leaders to attend and stressing the urgency of joint withdrawal of occupation forces so that Koreans could solve their own problems. Hodge and southern right-wing politicians ridiculed this proposal for a North-South Conference as a Communist ruse to seize the entire country.[6] North Korea did not consult either Kim Kyu-sik or Kim Gu before issuing its invitations, leaving the Korean leaders facing a difficult dilemma. Attendance would lend legitimacy to a constitution that North Korea had prepared for discussion. On the other hand, the leaders had proposed the conference. More important, both Kims were committed nationalists who knew that the Soviets would repeat separate elections in the north and thereby solidify Korea's arbitrary border.[7]

Before accepting North Korea's invitation, the Kims sent a liaison team to the northern capitol at Pyongyang on April 7 to discuss terms for attending the conference. During three days of lengthy conversations, Kim Il Sung and Kim Du-bong appeared determined to secure the attendance of the two Kims. North Korea's leaders promised that the Soviets would not participate, the agenda would be open for discussion, and there would be no pressure to ratify their draft constitution. Furthermore, the conference would not operate as an all-Korean assembly; southern representatives would have safe passage; a second meeting would convene in Seoul to finalize any agreements; and a few southern reporters could cover the proceedings. Kim Kyu-sik and Kim Gu still hesitated. A U.S. military government campaign to discredit the Kims increased their motivation to attend. American officials denounced Kim Kyu-sik as a "dupe" of Moscow who had no significant popular support and had personal advancement as a main motive. More important, the Kims had linked their political fate to the conference. Kim Kyu-sik, for example, had resigned as chair of the SKILA to protest the existence of separate elections, which he knew Rhee and the Korean Democratic Party would control. Finally, UNTCOK's Australian and Canadian delegates encouraged the Kims to attend the conference, telling them that the commission would reconsider its decision if the conference proposed an alternative to elections. On April 19 and 21, Kim Kyu-sik and Kim Gu, respectively, left for Pyongyang.[8]

Just before he left for Pyongyang, Kim Kyu-sik issued a statement containing five principles, which the North Korean leaders accepted as a basis for discussion:

1. Any form of dictatorship shall be rejected, and a truly democratic government should be established.
2. Monopolistic capitalism shall be rejected, and private ownership should be recognized.
3. A unified central government shall be established through a general election of the entire nation.
4. No military bases shall be allowed for any foreign power.
5. Regarding the early withdrawal of the two occupation forces, the powers concerned should immediately open negotiations for reaching an agreement as to the time and conditions of withdrawal and make a definite pronouncement to the world.

A strong anti-Communist, Kim undoubtedly hoped that the five principles would help preserve democracy if the Koreans succeeded in forming a coalition government at the conference. Another request sought clarification of the purpose of the North Korean People's Army (KPA), composed, he alleged, of "800,000 trained men who are seasoned fighters, part of which number may sweep down at any moment and organize a Soviet Government in South Korea." Kim Kyu-sik opposed immediate withdrawal without a guarantee from the north not to invade. As a deterrent, he urged the U.S. military government to recruit and train a defensive force of 200,000 to 300,000 soldiers.[9]

On April 19, the conference opened at Pyongyang's Moranbong Theatre. Three days later, the two Kims met privately with their hosts at a Pyongyang hotel, as follows:

> It was about 10:00, after having breakfast. Kim Il Sung and Kim Du-bong came to the Sangu-ri Hotel. Kim Il Sung, with his hair combed straight back, greeted Kim Kyu-sik by saying that it must have been difficult to make such a long trip. Kim kept combing his hair back with his fingers as loose strands kept falling on his forehead. He was tall and had a husky voice. His hands were very big, more than twice the size of an average person's. Soon Kim Gu went to the Moranbong Theatre. Kim Kyu-sik did not go, excusing himself because of sickness. He said he had come to negotiate, not to attend the joint conference.

When Kim Gu and two companions entered the conference hall, 545 representatives from 16 political parties and 40 social organizations were present, but only about 50 were from southern Korea. They were greeted with loud applause, which encouraged them in their belief that the border dividing Korea was artificial. Kim Il Sung delivered a long speech that hailed progress toward democratic reconstruction in the north, criticized repression in the south, and condemned the United States for blocking reunification. He concluded with a call to "shatter the American plot to colonize South Korea" and "to save the fatherland from the urgent danger facing it ... by destroying the May 10 election."[10]

Kim delivered a short speech to the conference delegates, calling on those in attendance to put aside differences and oppose the May 10 elections:

> I am greatly honored to attend such a great meeting where patriots from the South and North are gathered to discuss a great plan for achieving unified independence. Without the fatherland, there is no nation; without the nation, there is no party, no ideology, no group. The greatest task of our whole nation is to achieve unified independence. The biggest hindrance, right now, is the separate election. Therefore, our common goal should be to shatter the separate election and the separate government.[11]

Kim's optimism quickly proved unwarranted. During the next two sessions, various parties submitted statements to the planning committee. The statements were read aloud in open session, and the delegates voted on each by a show of hands without discussion or debate. Approval of these statements came amid silence, hiding whatever opposition existed behind the unanimous adoption of three resolutions.[12] Predictably, the first statement attacked the United States for sabotaging efforts to achieve reunification, blamed Rhee and the UN for colluding in an "American scheme" to colonize Korea, lauded South Koreans for their patriotic struggle, and vowed to block the elections and to secure withdrawal of foreign troops from Korea. The second resolution appealed directly to a nationalist belief that there was only one Korea. It urged a "national salvation struggle" because

> executing the election under open foreign interference is a treasonous plot of the country-selling band of Syngman Rhee and Kim Song-su, who have betrayed our country from long before, wagging their tails in front of the American imperialist plunderers, and who want to establish a government of country-destroying traitors to carry out the American imperialists' wicked plot. But under no circumstances will it be possible. Koreans are not dead. Our people are unified and there is only one fatherland. No real Korean, whoever he is, will ever recognize such a government.... If we hesitate, even a bit, at this critical moment of danger for our fatherland, what will happen to our descendants and how greatly will they

blame us! Our descendents will curse the bastards who are helping to divide our land and colonize it once again.

Implementing a third resolution, a "struggle committee" drafted a letter to the Soviet and American commanders that all 56 political groups (41 from the south) attending the conference signed, but the two Kims did not. First, it demanded that the UNTCOK stop the elections and leave Korea. Second, it requested Soviet-American withdrawal so that Koreans could "solve their own national problems" by means of free nationwide elections.[13]

Although the conference adjourned on April 23, informal meetings continued for another week. The four Kims met on the morning of April 30, resulting in a decision for one representative from each political party and social group at the conference to attend a South-North Leaders' Conference that afternoon. This meeting resulted in the adoption of a statement restating opposition to separate elections. At the end of the conference on April 30, a joint communiqué was issued, signed by the representatives of North and South Korean political parties and social organizations. The political program advanced in this communiqué had three premises. First, the only solution for the Korean problem under existing conditions was immediate and simultaneous withdrawal of foreign troops from Korea. Second, leaders of both North and South Korea had to state that they would never permit an outbreak of civil war or any disturbance that might block fulfillment of the Korean desire for unity after foreign troops withdrew. Third, after such withdrawal, a political conference of all Korea would convene to form a "democratic provisional government." On the principles of universal, direct, and equal suffrage and on the basis of a secret ballot, this body would then elect a United Korean Legislative Organ, which in turn would formulate and adopt a constitution. Last, political parties and social groups signing this statement stated that they never would accept the outcome of a separate election in South Korea or the resultant government. The next day, the southern delegates attended May Day celebrations in Pyongyang, watching thousands parading through the banner-decked streets carrying signs opposing separate elections and praising the conference.[14]

On returning to Seoul on May 5, Kim Kyu-sik and Kim Gu issued a statement that North Korean authorities had pledged never to establish a separate government. Kim Kyu-sik told an UNTCOK member, "Kim Il Sung had proposed the clause about no civil war and he had no reason to distrust it."[15] Anticipating an end to Korea's arbitrary division, most southerners at first were enthusiastically optimistic, and the prestige of the Kims soared. The southern delegates reported favorably on conditions in the north and testified to the moderate opinions and unqualified patriotism of the North Korean leaders. Hodge quickly implemented a vigorous campaign to discredit those who had attended the North-South Conference, labeling them as Communist dupes. His determination to hold a separate election on schedule caused the Kims to retreat. Kim Gu declared that while he did not favor the elections, he opposed imposition of the northern system on the south. Kim Kyu-sik said that he no longer would work openly against the elections. To reduce the number of people voting, Radio Pyongyang announced that the Soviet Union, in response to the request of the North-South Conference, had agreed to withdraw its troops by the end of the year.[16]

Moderates were no longer a viable political force in South Korea after the North-South Conference. The failure to develop a plan for removal of the artificial border at the thirty-eighth parallel accelerated the political polarization in the American zone. Subsequent developments completed the process. Less than two weeks after the two Kims spoke positively about North Korea's intentions, Pyongyang suddenly cut the supply of electricity to South Korea, after promising not to do so. This action, probably designed to scuttle the elections, generated intense resentment among South Koreans and discredited Kim Kyu-sik and Kim Gu. Right-wing groups charged the participants in the North-South Conference with duplicity, ridiculing their promise as nothing but a trick to deceive the people. On May 10, 1948, southern Koreans elected 200 representatives to a "national" assembly for the ROK, leaving 100 seats open for future northern delegates. That summer, the legislature met and elected Rhee as the ROK's president, who immediately declared his commitment to "March North."[17]

Meanwhile, the two Kims and their supporters had held a series of meetings that resulted in a decision to postpone further direct efforts for North-South collaboration until after the elections. Less than two weeks before elections in the south, the North Korean People's Committee adopted a new constitution purporting to apply to all of Korea. In late June, Kim Il Sung and Kim Du-bong invited Kim Kyu-sik and Kim Gu to attend another conference at Haeju, just north of the thirty-eighth parallel, to plan for nationwide elections. Their response reportedly was to propose that the North Koreans arrange for election of 100 representatives to serve in the new National Assembly. Other southerners who had participated in the April conference declined to attend and issued a declaration denouncing this second conference as both illegal and contrary to northern promises not to form a separate government. When it convened on June 29, North Koreans dominated the new joint conference. On July 5, delegates voted not to recognize the South Korean Assembly. Instead, they approved a national election on August 25 to establish a "Korea's Supreme People's Assembly" to represent all Koreans.[18]

Tragically, Japan's defeat in World War II left Korea not liberated, but artificially divided. Thereafter, negotiations among the Koreans themselves to achieve reunification ended in failure. The North-South Conference was unlikely to achieve reunification, not least because of the presence of foreign troops. Despite the international origins of the arbitrary boundary dividing the peninsula, domestic factors had begun to reinforce the line as a permanent border. On the eve of inauguration of the ROK, a South Korean group made a final attempt to promote joint North-South collaboration. On August 3, 18 members of the newly elected National Assembly introduced a resolution calling for creation of a "special unification committee" to explore all avenues for removing the arbitrary border at the thirty-eighth parallel, but it met defeat. Almost a year later, any lingering hope for early reunification disappeared on June 26, 1949, with the assassination of Kim Gu. When the North Korean army occupied Seoul in June 1950, it captured Kim Kyu-sik, who later reportedly died in the north.[19] Leaders on both sides had the chance to create a united nation during the Korean War, but the armistice restored the division. Thereafter, the survival and strengthening of the arbitrary boundary across the peninsula would raise doubts about whether there would ever again be just one Korea.

2

Early Artificial Borders

Koreans proudly claim a united national history that began in the seventh century A.D. Before that time, shifting artificial borders had divided the Korean peninsula into a succession of contesting states that finally achieved stability during the Three Kingdoms Era, beginning in the fourth century A.D. Geography was a powerful force that combined with ethnic homogeneity to break down territorial divisions on the peninsula throughout Korea's history. Roughly the size of the state of Minnesota, Korea is 600 miles long and 200 miles wide, although it narrows to half that distance at the northern "neck" of the peninsula running from Pyongyang to Wonsan. To the west is the Yellow Sea and China, and to the east is the Sea of Japan, which Koreans call the East Sea. Since the Korean War ended in 1953, a 2.4-mile-wide DMZ has artificially divided the nation, with South Korea comprising 38,000 square miles and North Korea 47,000 square miles. Korea is a mountainous country; the Taebaek Range runs from the north down the center of the country, then along the east coast. Less than 20 percent of the land is arable, concentrated along river valleys. Although the north is more mountainous, the Chiri Range in the south represents a sharp contrast with the gentler terrain. There are 3,000 islands and islets, mostly off the western and southern coasts; the volcanic Cheju-do Island is the largest, at the country's southernmost point.[20]

Korea is the crossroads of Northeast Asia, which explains why historically it has been the target of invasion and foreign domination. In the north, it has a natural border with Russia extending 11 miles along the Tumen River and with China extending 636 miles along the Yalu (Amnok) River. For centuries, Chinese leaders referred to Korea as "a hammer ready to strike at the head of China." Japan's main island of Honshu is located only 60 miles to the east of Korea, and its Tsushima Island is visible in the Korea Strait. As a result, Japanese leaders have often called Korea "a dagger pointed at the heart of Japan." Korea's geographic link to the Asian heartland provides clues about the ethnic origins of its population. Anthropologists believe that people from Central Asia migrated to the Korean peninsula during prehistoric times, and there are traces of humans dating from the Paleolithic or Stone Age period, around 30,000 B.C. These hunters and gatherers showed increasing sophistication by 20,000 B.C., having formed settlements in river valleys and along the coasts at that time. A sedentary society emerged by roughly 6000 B.C. with organized agriculture that included grinding of grain and domestication of animals. Religion was a combination of animism (worship of natural objects) and shamanism (protection from evil spirits). The Bronze Age arrived around 232 B.C., a consequence of contact with China.[21]

Koreans constitute a unique ethnic group, the product of intermixture between the native inhabitants and assorted Manchurians, Mongolians, and Chinese who arrived over time. Their spoken language is distinctive, being polysyllabic and highly inflected with a wealth of adverbs and adjectives. Written Korean, or *Hangul*, is phonetic or constructed with letters, rather than pictographic, but artificial barriers could not prevent the borrowing of many words from Chinese. Korea also shares a creation myth with China and other East Asian nations. According to legend, around 4300 B.C. a bear and a tiger lived in a cave. Both wanted to become human and prayed to God for transformation. God told them to remain in the cave 1,000 days, but the impetuous tiger crossed the divine arbitrary boundary early. The patient bear stayed until the appointed moment and was transformed into a beautiful woman who married the son of heaven. The couple had a son named Tangun, who founded the first Korean state of Ko-Choson in 2333 B.C. and ruled for 1,000 years at the capital in Pyongyang. Of course, the story is apocryphal, but it does reveal how culture unites the people of East Asia in defiance of artificial borders.[22]

Korea's early civilization developed along its rivers, nearly all of which flow to the west or south. The Yalu River, constituting the northern border with China, is the longest and most navigable. The Taedong, Han, Kum, and Naktong rivers, located from north to south, respectively, are large with varied flow and generally poor navigation, except for the Taedong River. Records from the Eastern Zhou Dynasty after 1100 B.C. referred to people on the peninsula as the Tung-I. Confucius commented that Korea had a stable and orderly tribal society with fair taxation and effective rule. Chinese records established that the origin of Ko-Choson, the first identifiable Korean state, was in the fourth century B.C. "Choson" translates as "Morning Freshness" and gave rise to Korea's nickname, the "Land of the Morning Calm."

The Chinese obviously viewed the Yalu as an arbitrary border, staging military strikes across the river after 400 B.C. to assert dominance. This brought ancient Korea into contact for the first time with a sedentary and literate culture. Ko-Choson borrowed agricultural techniques to develop a thriving rice economy and a productive livestock industry. Soon, it showed expansionist ambitions northward, extending its control to the Liao River, until the Chinese state of Yen defeated Korea's armies in the early third century. In 221 B.C., the Chin Dynasty united China, imposing a brutal rule that spurred migration into Korea. Natural barriers between the two countries could not prevent contact with this superior culture, which caused disruption in Korea, a pattern that continued under the Han Dynasty.[23]

China's physical penetration of Korea led to the fall of Ko-Choson. In the early second century, the Korean king granted asylum to a fleeing Chinese rebel leader and his followers, who then organized a rebellion of the disaffected against the monarchy. Wei-man attacked and seized Pyongyang in 194 B.C., ousting the king and forcing him to flee to the south. His leadership and organization skills resulted in creation of a powerful tribal union that expanded trade with China under the Han Dynasty. In 109 B.C., however, China's Emperor Wu Ti led a land and sea assault against Korea, eliminating all resistance after a year of fighting. To rule Korea, he created four "commandaries" with entirely arbitrary borders, using his military forces to ensure control until A.D. 313. Four centuries of Chinese occupation accelerated the Korean embrace of Chinese civilization. Buddhism appeared in the sixth century and spread rapidly, supplanting local beliefs and superstitions. Countless temples and shrines were built. More significant was the arrival of Confucian philosophy, inculcating in the people notions of filial piety, loyalty to rulers, and emphasis on order and obedience.[24]

Artificial borders dominated the Three Kingdoms Era in Korean history, which dated from 37 B.C. to A.D 668. Late in the first century B.C., Koguryo had replaced Ko-Choson as the dominant state in northern Korea. Five tribes consisting of 30,000 to 80,000 families each had migrated to the peninsula from north of the Yalu River. Its warrior elite was at the top of a patriarchal society that forced the native population to pay tribute for land and defense. Koguryo's early leaders were anti-Chinese but benefited from contact with China to gain access to iron weapons and improve the economy through expanding trade. As Koguryo's military power grew, it became increasingly aggressive, waging constant warfare against its neighbors. Its forces even invaded and briefly occupied Beijing in A.D. 47. In 427, the kingdom moved its capitol to Pyongyang, which became the center of power, with elite homes, shrines, and temples. There also were warehouses for collection of taxes and tribute; a marketplace boosted regional commerce.[25]

Paekche, the second of Korea's Three Kingdoms, emerged in the southwestern part of the peninsula as a result of people migrating southward to escape Koguryo's rule. The superior technology of the new arrivals overwhelmed the native inhabitants. More important, the tribes composing Paekche maintained links with China from a capital city at Kwangju and even transmitted Chinese culture to Japan. Naturally, Paekche's leaders feared Koguryo because of its stronger economy, superior administrative organization, and historical claim as successor of Ko-Choson. There was rivalry and friction from the outset; Koguryo attacked Paekche first in A.D. 369. Three centuries of warfare followed at the Han River, which ran through Seoul in the middle of the peninsula. Paekche's strength derived from the adoption of Chinese institutions of government and society; it was free to do so because the authority of its leaders rested neither on tribal nor on kinship roots. There was evidence of democracy as well—the elite elected rulers to three-year terms, and major towns were self-governing with decision-making legislative bodies.[26]

The kingdom of Silla emerged in the southeast corner of Korea. Refugees fleeing warfare to the north in the early first century used superior technology to conquer the native Chin Han people in that region. Benefiting from isolation below the Sobaek mountain range, a confederation of six tribes had emerged by the early fourth century, but Silla remained politically weak and economically backward in comparison to both Koguryo and Paeckche. At the capitol of Kyongju, three families—Pak, Sok, and Kim—dominated the council of tribal leaders that governed the state and elected the king. Eventually, the Kim clan asserted hereditary claim to the throne. In 381, Silla sent its first embassy to Imperial China but developed closer ties with Koguryo based on the protection that its northern patron provided against Paekche. Periodic military threats from Japan across the East Sea transformed its status into that of quasi-protectorate. Silla drew strength from a kinship system that was at the center of its governmental structure, however. This provided for less erosion of Silla's customs and traditions, contributing to greater social cohesion and more lasting political power.[27]

Arbitrary boundaries were not just territorial but also cultural in the Three Kingdoms Era. Each state developed distinct qualities. Koguryo melded the strong influence of its nomadic Mongol past with native customs and Chinese traditions. Paekche's intimate relations with China promoted an imitative pattern that mirrored its patron's experience. Silla was the most individualistic state, drawing strength from a primitive simplicity. Silla's system of political and social stratification, known as the "bone ranks," provided a prime example. Based on lines of descent, there were three principal classes—*songgol* (sacred bone), *chingol* (true bone), and *tupum* (head rank). Kings held the first status, which claimed direct links to the original royal lineage of Pak. "Sacred bone" disappeared in the seventh century, after which all royalty belonged to the "true bone" class. Six classes composed "head rank," of which numbers six, five, and four constituted the aristocracy and ordinary people occupied the rest. Head rank status was a key consideration in appointment to important civil and military posts. It also dictated strict sumptuary regulations indicating a person's social status, including the style of housing, dress, means of transportation, and number of servants. Finally, the bone ranks set payments for tax and tribute.[28]

Buddhism was a force that weakened the borders separating the kingdoms after it arrived on the peninsula from China in the sixth century. The religion had a major impact on music, art, medicine, and architecture in all three states as well as fostering a nascent nationalism that broke down tribal loyalties. Silla's king used Buddhism as a political tool, establishing it as a state religion in A.D. 579. Confucianism also united the three kingdoms. The first school to teach this Chinese philosophy was established in Koguryo in A.D. 372, and creation of private academies for instruction of the aristocracy followed. Elite families embraced Confucianism in Paekche and Silla as well. The impact was to promote increased efficiency in the government of all three kingdoms, as each state adopted Confucian training for its officials and used the Chinese examination system to determine competence. Silla was slow to adopt the Chinese administrative model but recognized its benefits in A.D. 516, when it created a defense department, later adding departments of personnel, finance, and foreign affairs.[29]

By A.D. 400, Koguryo had established itself as a major regional power and held the initial advantage over its neighbors. King Kwanggaeto (391–413), the "achiever of great expansion," extended the state's control southward to the Han River and northward deep into Manchuria. Toward the end of the fifth century, King Changsu (413–491) assaulted Paekche and occupied Kwangju, capturing its king. Silla was already demonstrating increasing power, such as building a road network that linked all areas of the state. Its military operations pushed the state's border north to the Han River in 551 and then focused on conquest of Paekche, which never was a viable contestant in the competition to unite Korea. Beginning in 555, Silla systematically weakened Paekche with a series of attacks that by 589 had positioned it to eliminate its rivals. That year, the new Sui Dynasty in China began implementing an aggressive plan of expansion that would lead to sustained military operations against Koguryo in coordination with Silla. Surprisingly, Sui forces suffered a thorough and costly defeat in their final invasion attempt in 614. This disaster sparked a rebellion that brought the Tang Dynasty to power in China. Koguryo expected an invasion and built a huge wall north of the Yalu River after 630, which halted Tang forces in 645. Thereafter, the two sides fought a two-year war of attrition.[30]

China then implemented a new strategy that would lead to Korea's unification. In coordinated operations in 660, Tang naval and Silla land forces destroyed Paekche. Two years later, a dual military offensive crushed Koguryo in a pincer movement. Chinese occupation of Pyongyang in 668 marked elimination of arbitrary territorial boundaries and the birth of a united Korea. China, however, ignored Silla's demand to leave what it considered a barbarian tributary state. Determined to avert domination, Silla's military fought a series of fierce battles, which accomplished the complete ouster of Chinese forces in 676. This gave Silla firm control south of the peninsula's narrow neck. China under the Tang Dynasty acknowledged the tributary status of this area and finally recognized the autonomy of Silla in 735. From its beginning, however, Silla suffered from internal weakness because it was unable to reconcile absolutism with tribal authority. Elite landowners rebelled whenever the king attempted to expand his power. Violent clashes between tribal chiefs only added to an escalating pattern of chaos and anarchy. Freebooters and adventurers traded slaves and engaged in coastal piracy. In addition, Silla's economic progress created demands for greater access to political and social power.[31]

After conquering all of China, the Mongols targeted Korea in the 13th century, hoping to exploit the country's resources and prepare a route to invade Japan. Chingghis Khan, seen here, was one infamous Mongol chief, known for his ruthless and violent leadership style.

Silla collapsed in response to a mass rebellion in southwestern Cholla province in 892, where Kyon Hwon proclaimed himself king of "Later Paekche." The bandit Kung Ye became the leader of "Later Koguryo" in 901, but his preference for plunder and tyranny led to assassination of his successor in 918. General Wang Kon seized power and moved the capital to Kaesong, just above the thirty-eighth parallel, where he proclaimed the new state of Koryo. After initial military reversals, Wang Kon staged an offensive in 934 that resulted in occupation of Kyongju and abdication of the last Silla king. Two years later, destruction of later Paekche confirmed the triumph of Koryo. Wang Kon acted swiftly to extend Koryo's border north to the Yalu River in a symbolic demonstration of power and to expand trade. His policies achieved security and stability and created a foundation for his initial successors to reorganize the government, imitating the Chinese model. They failed, however, to break the power of the landowning elite and allowed ruthless exploitation of the peasantry.

Because of another threat from the Khitan Mongols north of the Yalu River, many fortresses and four walls were constructed by A.D. 987 to make permanent the arbitrary northern border of Korea. Koryo nevertheless remained stable for another two centuries, despite political decentralization and economic backwardness. Ultimately, in 1170, the extravagances of the scholar-official class angered an aggrieved military enough for two generals to stage a coup, which led to the emergence of a military dictatorship to rule Korea.[32]

Korea became a target for Chinggis Khan after complete conquest of China in 1279. Mongol forces overwhelmed the northern walls in 1219, but Koryo rejected their demands to pay tribute. An assault in 1231 met little resistance, resulting in imposition of military occupation and extraction of an immense annual tribute. The Mongols were most interested in exploiting Korean labor and resources to make possible invasion and conquest of Japan. After violent *kamakazi* ("divine wind") storms foiled two attempts, the Mongols after 1281 had to be satisfied with political domination, economic exploitation, and cultural repression in Korea.

Foreign rule sparked a revival of Korean nationalism. Rebellions in China against Mongol rule in 1350 encouraged

Koryo's puppet king to prepare to reassert native authority. With restoration of Chinese rule under the Ming Dynasty in 1368, King Kongmin immediately proposed formal relations and an alliance against the Mongols. Two years later, Yi Song-gye, his top general, initiated an offensive across the Yalu River, but the Koryo elite assassinated the king and regained power. In 1388, General Yi seized power, usurping the throne in 1392. Renaming his nation Choson, he moved the capitol to Seoul in 1395 and pledged *sadae* (serving the great) to China under the Ming Dynasty.[33]

Korea under the Yi Dynasty became a near clone of China in form. Five hundred years of close relations and loyalty, along with three tribute missions annually, bought protection at the price of subservience. Yi Song-gye distributed Koryo's royal lands to his "merit subjects" and used their support to eliminate the old landowning elite. He ruled as an absolute monarch in a government that replicated the Chinese model. The Choson Era was the heyday of Confucianism. A 1740 code provided for the recruiting of officials based on an examination system that tested mastery of Confucian philosophy. Only members of the *yangban* class, however, had access to the process, leading to a tiny self-perpetuating elite dominating the Yi bureaucracy. There also was an assault on Buddhism, which had gained inordinate economic and military power in the Koryo period.

Choson reached an apex of achievement under King Sejong (1418–1450), who developed a written language, issued a new law code, and provided tax relief for the peasantry. A patron of science, his efforts fostered technological advances that included rain and wind gauges, sundials and clocks, and use of movable type. His foreign policy expanded migration to new northern garrison towns and promoted trade with Japan. King Sejong's efficient rule promoted prosperity, stability, and the emergence of a modern national spirit that broke down the artificial borders perpetuating provincialism and regionalism in Korea.[34]

Choson's subsequent history revealed that its immature adaptation of the Chinese model failed to break down arbitrary social boundaries of the past. Defying monarchial power, the yangban acted together to elevate and protect their status, steadily increasing their landholdings and imposing immense burdens on the peasantry with grain taxes and forced labor. Factional competition revolving around the pretext of philosophical debate ensued, hiding a struggle for power, prestige,

YANGBAN

Yangban is the Korean name for the elite literati class that was at the apex of Korean society in the Choson period (1392–1905). Its existence, behavior, and impact provide a powerful example of how arbitrary social boundaries divided and weakened Korea during its early history. Below the yangban were the *chungin* (middle people), a heredity class of petty government officials unable to rise in the social order. Next were the *yangmin*, or "good people," composed of peasants who lived in isolated and self-governing villages. These commoners had to surrender half of their produce to yangban landowners and perform corvee (forced) labor for the state. At the bottom of the social order were the *chonmin* (base people), which included persons who were government industrial workers, butchers, actors, *kisaeng* ("skilled women"; the Korean version of Japanese geishas), vagrants, and slaves. At the apex of this social pyramid were the yangban, a name that literally means "two classes" or "groups."

Each day, at the king's dawn audience, there was the *panyol*, or "ordering by classes," when *munban* (civil class) stood in rows along the east side of the great courtyard and *muban* (military class) stood on the west side. Muban was always socially inferior to munban, but in time the court yangban title came to be applied to all who were eligible for government appointment, and it eventually became a polite way of referring to any gentleman.

Education in the Confucian classics was the single most distinguishing feature of the yangban class, and passage of an examination showing command of this knowledge was a qualification for office holding, although rural landholding and the resulting wealth also were inherited characteristics. Members of the class were exempt from corvee labor and military service. They propagated the principles of Confucian education, especially filial piety, as a means of strengthening their control over rural society, and their tenants and wealth that led to arrest, imprisonment, and execution of scores of Confucian officials. Meanwhile, Korea suffered astonishing economic deterioration. It had inferior roads, primitive communication, and little internal or external trade. Choson was entirely incapable of self-defense in 1587, when Japan's Hideyoshi Toyotomi requested passage through Korea

> in particular. Those who belonged to this elite class valued their own lineages, but blood ties did not define membership. Intense rivalry developed among the yangban based on lineage, region, office holding, and political opportunity. Although access to yangban status was difficult because it was heredity and was perpetuated behind an artificial social boundary from lower classes in Korean society, it was not homogeneous. Many yangban families were impoverished. Formerly excluded from office, illegitimate sons of yangban fathers, or those born to non-yangban mothers, ultimately gained recognition. Opportunities also increased for those outside the class to profit from trade and skills and then to acquire the education necessary to gain this elite status. The overall effect was therefore to broaden yangban membership and outlook, but without threatening its elite privileges.
>
> Broader than the Silla and Koryo elites, the yangban had land holdings scattered around the peninsula. This privileged elite dominated not only Korean society but also the government bureaucracy. These exalted scholar-officials occupied multiple posts, exploiting a hereditary monopoly over political power to enforce continuity and stability. Yangban created and defended rigid barriers to political, social, and economic reform to maintain dominance. There were prohibitions against marriage outside the class. Also, the yangban dictated cultural standards, setting strict guidelines for rites and ceremonies. Preservation of the economic status quo was another primary objective, not least because of a Confucian prejudice against commerce. The yangban imposed restrictions on trade relations and barriers to technological innovation. It was Korea's elite that constructed the "Hermit Kingdom" because this protected its class interests. Korea was incapable of defending itself against imperialist exploitation because the yangban had created artificial borders promoting social stagnation, political inefficiency, and economic backwardness.

to conquer China. With factionalism preventing a definitive reply, Hideyoshi launched an invasion in 1592 and occupied Seoul in three weeks. Koreans attribute Japan's ultimate defeat to famous Admiral Yi Sun-sin, who deployed ironclad "turtleships" to intercept Japanese supply ships, but other factors were more important. China under the Ming Dynasty sent an army that joined Korean guerrillas and armed Buddhist monks to force the retreat of Japanese invaders already battling cold weather, malnutrition, and disease. After peace negotiations failed, Japan sent reinforcements in 1597, but a Chinese offensive and Hideyoshi's death in 1598 ended the costly adventure.[35]

For Korea, Japan's invasion was an unmitigated national disaster. Uncontrolled fires and indiscriminate plunder laid waste to temples, towns, and treasures. Cultivation of land fell by two-thirds, and Japan extracted harsh tribute during its occupation. Corrupt officials exploited the distress to destroy land registers, making it possible for the yangban to seize more property. Then, before recovery was complete, the Manchu campaign to replace the Ming Dynasty in China after 1625 led to another invasion of Korea. After ten years of war, Manchu forces eliminated all resistance and compelled Korea's surrender in 1637. Choson forces then joined the Manchu offensive that destroyed the Ming Dynasty in 1644. By then, Korea was in shambles. The traumatic impact of dual invasions turned the attention of Koreans inward, reflecting an intense fear of outside contacts. Yi edicts achieved a self-imposed isolation, closing tightly the northern border, prohibiting outside travel and visitors, and allowing trade only with China and Japan. China's Qing Dynasty handled Korea's foreign relations. All these artificial boundaries enhanced the ability of the yangban to pursue personal gain in disregard of the nation's interest. After 1700, the yangban became obsessed with constructing genealogies to determine family origin and social rank. Once linked to royalty, a promising son might become king and advance his family's fortunes. A dysfunctional political system stayed in place into the 1800s.[36]

Korea's early history provides instructive insights into the impact of arbitrary boundaries in human history. First, the Three Kingdoms Era showed how territorial divisions could encourage even a homogenous people to develop distinctively different political, social, and economic systems of state organization in the same land. Second, unification of the Korean peninsula under Silla and later Koryo demonstrated the power of nationalism as a force to break down artificial barriers that hampered commercial and cultural interaction. Third, the Mongol conquest of Korea was part of an overall plan aimed at eliminating the borders standing in the way of its vision of a united Asian empire. Koreans drew strength from a belief in the benefits of boundaries as a means to preserve and protect not only national sovereignty but also ethnic identity, traditional customs, and cultural values. Fourth, the Yi Dynasty successfully established artificial borders that closed Choson to the outside world, promoting peace and apparent stability. Inside Korea, however, progress and modernization undermined the arbitrary boundaries that restricted social, economic, and political advancement, as merchants and intellectuals in particular demanded their removal. Finally, Korea's early history hinted at how interaction between nations in the modern world would make the survival of arbitrary boundaries almost impossible.

3

Imperialist Impositions

Korea at the start of the nineteen century had escaped serious notice outside of Northeast Asia. Westerners familiar with the peninsular nation referred to it as the Hermit Kingdom. Indifference allowed Korea to maintain its isolation from the outside world without the need to protect its territorial borders, whereas its more artificial social, cultural, and economic boundaries remained immune to change. At first, Korea could look to China for protection against outside penetration; in addition, it was a less inviting target for Western commercial expansion. Great Britain's effortless victory over China in the First Opium War opened all of East Asia to Western imperialist penetration after 1840. The Treaty of Nanjing showed that the Middle Kingdom was backward and vulnerable because of an absence of economic modernization and an ineffective government. After the Taiping Rebellion rocked China in 1854, China was defeated again in the Second Opium War, which began in 1856, resulting in the signing of the Treaty of Tianjin. Imposition of the unequal treaties on China would be the prelude for territorial dismemberment during the 1890s. In the meantime, China's tributary states had become fair game for subjection to foreign domination. With Great Britain concentrating on Malaya, France on Indochina, and the Netherlands on Indonesia, Russia and Japan clashed for control over Korea.

Historians have referred to the nineteenth century as the Age of Imperialism. There were at least three motives behind Europe's pursuit of colonies in Africa, Asia, and the Mideast. First, industrialization had taken hold in Europe, resulting in increased production of manufactured goods. As competitors raised tariff barriers to protect domestic markets, producers looked for consumer outlets overseas. Second, burgeoning nationalism encouraged competition among European states. Adding psychological power to this contest was application of Charles Darwin's theory of evolution to social organization, which persuaded many governments that large military establishments, overseas naval bases, and colonies reflected a nation's superiority. Third, racist ethnocentrism caused many Europeans to believe that they had a sacred duty to uplift backward people and spread the blessings of economic, social, and political progress worldwide. The belief was what Rudyard Kipling labeled the "white man's burden," which included spreading religion. Convinced that it was their duty to save backward people from damnation, Protestant and Catholic missionaries traveled to Asia and Africa to convert heathens to Christianity.[37]

Imperialism was a powerful force in the nineteenth century, assaulting artificial barriers everywhere in East Asia. At first, it spared Korea, in part because the Yi rulers had turned Choson inward and established rigid arbitrary borders to isolate it from the outside world. Until the 1870s, imperialist nations showed little interest in the country known as the "Land of the Morning Calm." Earlier contacts were accidental. Dutch seamen in the early seventeenth century were the first visitors to Korea from the West, venturing inland to secure water and supplies or after shipwreck forced them ashore. Great Britain displayed a brief interest in developing trade ties in the early nineteenth century, but Choson twice refused to negotiate a commercial treaty. In 1847, a typhoon destroyed three French frigates off Korea's coast, ending their efforts to establish contacts. When Russia sent representatives to Seoul in 1866, Korea directed them to Beijing, explaining that Korea was a dependency of China. Acting on this premise, France approached the Qing Dynasty but was rebuffed. "Though Korea is a dependent country of China, it is not a territorial possession," the Chinese replied, and "hence in its domestic and foreign affairs, it is self-governing."[38]

In 1855, four American crewmen of the whaler *Two Brothers* who had jumped ship washed ashore on the east coast of Korea near Wonsan. Korean villagers cared for them until authorities in Seoul transported them to China en route back to the United States.[39] Choson's isolation remained intact.

Korea also escaped the concentrated attention of Christian missionaries, learning about Catholicism from China through emissaries and tribute missions. In fact, the first missionary in

Choson was Zhou Wen-mu, a Chinese Christian. The Yi Dynasty showed a firm determination to defend its arbitrary boundary against contact with the rest of the world in the hostile way it responded to the arrival of Christianity. For many suffering Koreans, this Western religion helped them endure economic destitution. The appeal of Catholicism was limited to a few provinces, but the number of conversions rose late in the century. The Yi government prohibited Christianity in 1786 because Confucianism demanded ancestor worship and the foreign creed threatened state control. Vigorous persecution started after 1800 with the banning of Christian books as subversive. Execution of Zhou Wen-mu for treason in 1801, however, did not deter French priests from sneaking into Choson in 1836. For another generation, the Christian missionary movement concentrated on China because Korea was hundreds of miles north of its base at Guangzhou.[40]

Choson would be incapable of defending itself when imperialist apathy toward the Hermit Kingdom ended. By 1800, the Yi Dynasty had entered a period of accelerated decline, with the arbitrary boundaries that had maintained stability crumbling. There was growing domestic disruption because social stratification was breaking down. Royal artisans were now private craftsmen. Rich peasants were gaining more land and wealth, which allowed them and wealthy merchants to buy yangban status and escape taxation. At the same time, many yangban now were impoverished. This group, as well as younger yangban denied government office, joined in a revolt among intellectuals who rejected the rituals and empty formalism of Confucianism. They embraced *sirhak*, or "practical learning," from the West, demanding government reorganization, land reform, and equal rights. Equally as destabilizing were wretched conditions in rural Choson, where destitution ravaged the countryside. In 1784, a combination of drought, flood, pestilence, and epidemic caused the deaths of 500,000 people from starvation. Thousands of beggars and vagrants joined unorganized mobs, which soon engaged in rampant banditry and lawlessness. During 1811 and 1812, organized peasant uprisings protested taxation and corrupt officials.[41]

Abject misery reenergized the appeal of Christianity among Koreans. In 1839, the Yi government reacted with repression, executing three French priests and arresting, imprisoning, and killing converts. Fears of a repeat of European retribution after the First Opium War ended the campaign, resulting in an estimated 20,000 Koreans converting to Catholicism over the next two decades. This contributed to the onset of a new age of antiforeign reaction in Choson. In 1863, Kojong became king at the age of 12 years. Until he reached maturity in 1873, the Taewongun, "Grand Prince," (1821–1898), who was his father, ruled as regent. A militant proponent of tradition, he sought restoration of a golden age and in 1866 renewed persecution of Christians, resulting in arrest and execution of foreign priests and the massacre of 18,000 Korean converts. Expecting retaliation, he formed a 12,000-person army with modern arms and supervised construction of new coastal defenses. Taewongun also acted to strengthen the monarchy, compelling the yangban to pay taxes and recruiting officials outside the elite. In October 1866, France's punitive expedition of seven ships and 600 soldiers arrived at Kanghwa Island on the west coast near Seoul. Acting on the Taewongun's orders, a local official demanded the immediate departure of this expedition. Ignoring this arbitrarily drawn line in the sand, French forces proceeded to loot and burn the town on Kanghwa; three were killed and 30 wounded.[42]

In August of that year, Koreans had clashed with the American schooner *General Sherman* when the vessel sailed into a rain-swollen Taedong River and moved toward the city of Pyongyang in search of trade. The Yi government issued orders that the *General Sherman* was to depart Korea at once, threatening to destroy the ship and execute its crewmen, composed mostly of Chinese and Malays. Immediate departure, however, was not possible because the Taedong's water level had fallen, leaving the *General Sherman* hopelessly stuck in the mud of the river's bed. Enraged Koreans attacked and burned the vessel, killing six crewmen who survived the assault and tried to surrender. Undaunted, the United States in 1869 instructed Frederick F. Low, the U.S. minister to China, to travel to Korea to negotiate a navigation and trade treaty. In May 1871, Low arrived at the port city of Chemulpo aboard the U.S.S. *Colorado*, but Korean emissaries rejected his request for a treaty. In June, while Low waited, Korean batteries delivered cannon fire to U.S. gunboats and steamships, whose officers and crewmen were exploring Kanghwa.[43]

Low adamantly opposed retreat. "In estimating the effect it may exert upon our power and prestige, which will affect the interests of our people in the East," he advised Washington, "the situation must be viewed from the oriental stand-point, rather than the more advanced one of Christian civilization."[44] Should the squadron sail away, it would embolden both Koreans and Chinese to commit more antiforeign excesses. Receiving approval, Low led a punitive operation against the Koreans that one historian has called the First Korean War. On June 10, 1871, Low's flotilla moved against Kanghwa Island, carrying two companies of marines and another of sailors armed with rifles. Assaulting Korean fortifications, U.S. forces applied stern punishment to the hopelessly outgunned Koreans. After gunboat bombardment, the marines and sailors assaulted enemy positions, shooting and burning. The punitive expedition destroyed five forts and killed about 250 Koreans; three Americans died and three were wounded. Violence had failed to gain what diplomacy could not, as the Koreans refused to negotiate. In July, Low and the U.S. flotilla left.[45]

Korea's early encounters with France and the United States encouraged the Yi government's belief that the artificial borders that it had created would guarantee protection. "Another of the great powers of the West has been humbled," the Taewongun said after Low's retreat. "Korea has shown her great patron China how to handle the barbarians."[46] Not only did Choson reaffirm its policy of refusing to negotiate, but also religious repression and seclusion continued. For example, in 1868, the Taewongun

Kojong, seen here, was king of Korea from 1864–1907, during a period in world history known as the Age of Imperialism. Throughout his reign, multiple countries fought to claim authority over Korea, causing political dissent and several military conflicts.

ignored a mission that Japan had sent to establish diplomatic and commercial relations, arrogantly dismissing his neighbor as a cultural inferior. He reiterated this position in 1872, when Japan asked for representation in Seoul. Rejection of a renewed request in 1873, when the regency ended, resulted in Japan's formulation of plans for an invasion. Koreans fired on a Japanese survey expedition in 1875, prompting Tokyo to send warships, which leveled the fort on Kanghwa Island. The next year, a Japanese mission traveled to Beijing to demand that China end Korea's tributary relationship with the Qing Dynasty. Reflecting its weakness, China agreed to broker a settlement, compelling Choson to sign the Treaty of Kanghwa in February 1876. This agreement removed the artificial barriers to political access in Korea, recognizing it as an independent state and providing for it to exchange diplomatic envoys with Japan.[47]

China's Li Hongzhang then devised a strategy to maintain Chinese preeminence in Korea. He encouraged the United States to open trade relations with Choson as a way to check Japan's ambition to dominate the peninsula. U.S. Commodore Robert W. Shufeldt, only too happy to oblige, sailed to Chemulpo. On May 22, 1882, he signed the first treaty between Korea and a Western nation, providing for peace, amity, commerce, and navigation. The first article of the Treaty of Chemulpo was the most important. It provided, "if other powers deal unjustly or oppressively with either Government, the other will exert their good offices, on being informed of the case, to bring about an amicable arrangement, thus showing their friendly feelings." Lucius H. Foote, the first U.S. minister to Korea, made it possible for a delegation of Koreans to visit the United States. At the request of King Kojong, he offered advice to Korea's government on a variety of matters. Foote also arranged for two American trading firms to operate in Korea, for another to gain a lease on a gold mine, and for Thomas Edison to secure an exclusive franchise to install electric light and telephone systems. Horace N. Allen, Foote's resident physician, opened a hospital and staffed it with medical missionaries. Ignoring Korean law, he worked to convert Koreans to Protestantism.[48]

Great Britain, France, and Germany also signed treaties with Korea to secure the same rights as the United States. Russia and Japan, however, had greater imperial ambitions on the Korean peninsula, which would lead to war and the imposition of a new arbitrary boundary, closing Korea to the outside world. At first,

Tokyo viewed Beijing as its main rival in Korea, meddling in Yi politics to promote a faction that favored modernization following the Japanese model. The Taewongun, who lost power when King Kojong reached maturity, staged a coup in July 1882 that resulted in a mob burning Japan's legation and killing seven Japanese military officers. Desperate to preempt Tokyo, China sent a large force to arrest the Taewongon and imprisoned him in China. Beijing then exploited its advantage by imposing a new treaty on Korea that gave China sweeping advisory, military, and economic power. According to Li Hongzhang, "I am king of

TREATY OF CHEMULPO

The Treaty of Chemulpo, the first between Korea and a Western nation, eliminated the arbitrary boundary that the Yi Dynasty had established around Korea to isolate it from the outside world. It also drew the United States into the rivalry for control of the Korean peninsula, which involved Russia, Japan, and China, near the end of the nineteenth century. Koreans later pointed to this treaty to justify charges of U.S. betrayal when Washington sanctioned Japanese annexation of Korea in the Taft-Katsura Agreement of 1905 and the Root-Takahira Agreement of 1908. Commodore Robert W. Shufeldt set the stage for the treaty when he visited Japan and China in the spring of 1880. He visited Li Hongzhang, the powerful viceroy of Zhili, who offered to make Shufeldt a grand admiral in the Chinese navy after Shufeldt had returned to the United States. Shufeldt returned to China but came authorized to negotiate a treaty to open Korea, an objective he had pursued since investigating the *General Sherman* incident in 1867.

Although Li extended considerable social and military courtesies, accompanying Shufeldt on tours of inspection of forts and naval vessels and lavishing attention on his adopted daughter (and niece) Molly Miller, who was Shufeldt's social hostess, the commodore was caught between the competing Chinese and Japanese efforts to control Korea and the power struggle in the Korean court. Eventually, King Kojong's intervention in favor of negotiations would lead to the sending of a Korean envoy and 70-man trading mission to Tianjin to discuss the possibility of a treaty with the United States.

Korea whenever I think the interests of China require me to assert that prerogative."

Two years later, pro-Japanese Koreans broke into the palace, burned buildings, captured Kojong, and murdered his pro-China advisors. Chinese troops soon overwhelmed the rebels, reasserting dominance over the government for another decade. In 1894, Japan exploited a religious uprising in Korea to maneuver China into deploying troops. This provided a pretext for Tokyo to send ships containing 8,000 soldiers to Chemulpo; the soldiers occupied the palace in Seoul and captured Kojong.

> After receiving new instructions from Washington to negotiate, Shufeldt worked with Li over the next six months to draft an agreement.
>
> Both Li Hongzhang and Yixin, head of Chinese foreign affairs, wanted an article inserted into the U.S.-Korean treaty indicating that "Chosen" (Korea) was a dependency of China. When the commodore requested guidance, Washington was silent, but Shufeldt persisted. After leaving Tianjin, he took what would become the Treaty of Chemulpo to Korea for signing on May 22, 1882, escorted by Chinese warships from Li's north naval squadron. The agreement omitted the dependency clause but was accompanied by an exchange of letters between King Kojong and U.S. President Chester A. Arthur that affirmed it. Also known as the Shufeldt Treaty, its provisions permitted U.S. citizens to trade and erect residences and warehouses in the open ports; set a tariff of 10 percent on necessities, 30 percent on luxuries, and 5 percent on exports; guaranteed rights to victims of shipwrecks; provided for reciprocal diplomatic and consular representatives; prohibited the opium trade; and granted the United States extraterritorial jurisdiction and most-favored-nation privileges. Most important, the United States promised to extend its "good offices" if Korea became involved in a dispute with another country.
>
> Thereafter, a succession of American diplomats, beginning with Lucius H. Foote as the first U.S. ambassador, would assert that Korea was independent of China. This accorded with Japanese sentiments at the time to support those in the Korean court resisting Chinese claims of suzerainty. It also led the United States and Japan to cooperate in resisting Li's doomed attempts to keep Korea within the Chinese orbit.

Japan insisted on administrative reforms and ignored Chinese demands to withdraw.[49]

China's declaration of war on Japan ignited a conflict in which Japanese forces scored easy and complete victories at sea and on land in Korea and Manchuria. In April 1895, the treaty ending the Sino-Japanese War forced China to pay an indemnity and to transfer Taiwan to Japan, along with abandoning all claims to authority over Korea. No sooner had Japan begun to enact measures for modernization and to assert dominance in Korea than Russia accelerated an existing plan for economic and political penetration of that nation. Queen Min, Kojong's mother and an ardent traditionalist, sought Russian support to oust Japan. In October 1895, the Japanese administrator allowed disaffected Koreans to storm the palace and murder her. Russia immediately deployed 200 soldiers in Seoul to restore law and order, as well as providing Kojong with asylum in its legation for more than a year. Russia now was the dominant force in Korea, a dramatic reversal that Japan patiently waited to rectify, in the meantime expanding its military capabilities in preparation for war. It also tried compromise. In June 1896, the world's diplomats gathered to celebrate Tsar Nicholas II's coronation at St. Petersburg. Japan's Yamagata Aritomo proposed dividing Korea at the thirty-eighth parallel, but Russia refused.[50] Russia's aggressiveness set off a scramble for economic concessions in 1897 that "divided China like a melon" as the imperialist powers created artificial borders to protect their spheres of influences.[51]

Imperialist impositions on Korea discredited the Yi government and gave birth to internal political dissent. In 1896, So Chae-pil (Philip Jaisohn) returned from studying in the United States and formed the Independence Club (*Tongnip Hyophoe*). An embryonic Korean political party, the first issue of its newspaper proclaimed a platform of "Korea for the Koreans, clean politics, the cementing of foreign friendships." So initiated a mass campaign for reform aimed at ending corruption and maladministration. Among his most vocal supporters was Yi Sung-man (Syngman Rhee) (1875–1965), who helped

After its 1905 victory in the Russo-Japanese War, Japan placed imperial control on Korea. Like England, the United States, and other leading nations at the turn of the century, Japan wanted to seize authority in underdeveloped countries to spread its influence and increase its economic advantages over other world powers. Here, Japanese soldiers control crowds in Korea in 1910.

organize mass demonstrations in 1896 decrying the foreign threat and demanding action to assert independence. The Independence Club condemned any limits on sovereignty, criticizing King Kojong for granting economic privileges to Russia and staying in its legation. In February 1897, the king finally moved into a new royal palace. Popular agitation and protest also forced Russia to retreat, foreswearing a large concession, closing a bank controlling government finance, and withdrawing troops. The Yi government saw the Independence Club as a threat to the artificial barriers that it had created to preserve its power, prompting the suppression of dissidents and forcing them underground in 1898. There might have been a mass rebellion had the Independence Club tried to mobilize the peasantry.[52]

Russia ignored the Korean dissidents and pressed for total control after signing a joint protectorate agreement in June 1896 that limited troop deployment with Japan. It sent advisors to supervise military reorganization and exercise military control in time of war. Early in 1903, Russian troops arrived on the Trans-Siberian Railroad and moved to establish occupation of northwest Korea. In June, Japan delivered a final offer to Russia proposing recognition of Russian hegemony in Manchuria in return for Japanese dominance over Korea. Russia's inflexible rejection reflected the confident expectation of an easy victory in a war that began in February 1904 with Japan's surprise sea attack on the Russian naval base at Port Arthur in Manchuria. To the world's surprise, the Japanese army and navy destroyed Russia's military units on land and at sea. As for Korea, Japan had moved troops into Korea in advance. Three weeks after the war began, Tokyo compelled Kojong to accept a protocol that made Korea a virtual vassal of Japan. Yet the Japanese triumph had come at the price of increasing economic and financial strain. Unable to invade and conquer Russia, Tokyo asked U.S. President Theodore Roosevelt to mediate a peace agreement. In September 1905, the Treaty of Portsmouth, which ended the Russo-Japanese War, provided, "Russia, recognizing that Japan has predominant political, military, and economic interests in Korea, agrees not to interfere or place obstacles in the way of any measure of direction, protection, and supervisions which the Imperial Government of Japan may deem necessary to adopt in Korea."[53]

Japan's imposition of imperialist control on Korea in 1905 was just one example of a global pattern that was in place as the twentieth century began. Powerful nations had been establishing arbitrary borders in underdeveloped nations to delineate territorial spheres of influence, where they could practice exclusive economic exploitation. At the same time, the governments of these nations were using tariffs to close internal markets and protect domestic industries. Creation of artificial barriers at home and abroad had emerged as a profound force determining events in the modern world. The United States had tried to reverse this trend with its announcement of the Open Door

Policy in 1899, calling for free trade and investment in China and later respect of its territorial integrity and political sovereignty. When the imperialist powers refused, the Americans joined the contest for spheres of economic, political, and military dominance abroad, as well, establishing its own colonial border around the Philippines. To win Japan's assent for this acquisition, the U.S. government withdrew its legation from Korea, prompting the other imperial powers to follow suit. This border-creating mentality motivated European nations over the next decade to align into two powerful military alliances. Hostility and suspicion would later ignite a world war to preserve and extend the arbitrary borders that these nations had created to impose and maintain Europe's hegemony around the globe.

in ways that served the Japanese Empire's strategic purposes. Colonization policies offered cheap land and transportation to relocate, and Japanese settlers flocked to Korea.[54]

European nations happily accepted Japan as a member of their imperialist club, not least because each saw this new Asian power as a potential ally in a future world war. For example, in August 1905, renewal of the Anglo-Japanese Alliance of 1902 included a provision that Great Britain would recognize Japan's paramount interests in Korea. Even the United States ignored its "good offices" obligations under the Treaty of Chemulpo and endorsed Japan's absorption of Korea in the Taft-Katsura Memorandum of July 1905 in return for recognition of U.S. control over the Philippines. President Theodore Roosevelt was more interested in maintaining friendly relations with Japan than in assisting Koreans, who soon were suffering not only from political repression but also from a severe agricultural depression. Those who could flee left Korea in what became a mass exodus. Many went to Hawaii to work as contract laborers, whereas others migrated to Mexico and California. Roosevelt, in 1907, closed U.S. borders to further Korean immigration. That year, King Kojong sought international help in restoring Korea's sovereignty with an appeal to the Hague Tribunal, but European leaders refused to hear his case. His effort infuriated Japan, resulting in his forced abdication. Under "The New Agreement" in August 1907, the resident general gained dictatorial powers, and his first act was to disband the Korean army.[55]

Koreans never forgave President Roosevelt for sanctioning Japanese domination, charging him with betrayal. Placing Korea behind Imperial Japan's artificial border served U.S. interests, however. "I should like to see Japan have Korea," Roosevelt wrote a friend in 1900. "She will be a check upon Russia, and she deserves it for what she has done." Racist attitudes reinforced his strategic calculations. Roosevelt was a great admirer of the war correspondent George Kennan, an uncle of the famous U.S. diplomat with the same name who in 1947 devised the containment policy. Covering the Russo-Japanese War for *The Outlook*,

Kennan had written several essays about Korea. In one, he wrote, "The average town Korean spends more than half his time in idleness, and instead of cleaning up the premises in his long intervals of leisure, he sits contentedly on his threshold and smokes, or lies on the ground and sleeps, with his nose over an open drain from which a turkey-buzzard would fly and a decent pig would turn away in disgust." In the fall 1905 issue of *The Outlook*, he compared "the cleanliness, good order, industry, and general prosperity" of Japan with "the filthiness, demoralization, laziness, and general rack and ruin" of Korea. Europeans shared Roosevelt's view that a racial divide explained Korean inferiority. After Washington closed its legation in Seoul, the U.S. vice consul likened the resultant exodus of foreign diplomats to a stampede of rats leaving a sinking ship.[56]

Mass resistance in Korea to Japanese impositions contradicted these derogatory assessments about Koreans. A nationwide network organized armed attacks and waged guerrilla warfare against Japanese soldiers. In 1908, rebel forces initiated 1,450 military engagements. Japan reacted with brutal repression, burning villages and killing 12,000 Koreans. Resistance plummeted but did not disappear. Failure of pacification created pressure in Japan to remove the remaining barriers to imperialist integration with outright annexation. Resident General Ito Hirobumi persuaded Tokyo to reject this option, but Korean patriot An Chung-gun assassinated him in October 1909 during a visit to Manchuria. On August 22, 1910, Korean officials transferred governmental power to Japan, and the last Yi monarch abdicated. Japan formally declared sovereignty over Korea and would rule the renamed "Chosen" under martial law as imperial administrators consolidated control. An initial focus on property ownership resulted in the conduct of a comprehensive survey and the immediate expropriation of five percent of all land. The government leased or managed most of it but sold some to absentee owners.[57]

An autonomous colonial administration under a governor general with unlimited powers ruled the Japanese colony of

Chosen. The chief agency for controlling the native populace was the omnipresent and oppressive Japanese police. To give the appearance of popular support, the governor general created in 1910 an "advisory council" composed of 65 Korean collaborators who provided advice on a limited range of issues. Resistance to colonial rule persisted, however, with fierce engagements between the imperial army and guerrillas occurring in the north. Korean rebels operated from sanctuaries in China and Russia, preventing Japanese forces from eliminating them entirely.

More dramatic in its impact was the March First (*Manse*) Rebellion in 1919—a campaign for liberation from Japanese rule that took place during negotiations at the Versailles Conference, the peace settlement after World War I. Japanese

MARCH FIRST MOVEMENT

The March First Movement sought the restoration of sovereignty and self-government in Korea after Japan had annexed the nation and placed it behind the arbitrary boundary of imperial rule. It received encouragement to a great extent from the principle of national self-determination that U.S. President Woodrow Wilson had been championing in World War I. The doctrine naturally appealed to the Korean people, who were suffering under harsh Japanese colonialism. Moreover, it provided the impetus to transform the Korean nationalist movement—a movement that had trusted in the activities of exiles and clandestine organizations—into a full-scale national effort to regain Korea's lost independence. This mass movement began when 33 "representatives of the Korean people" framed and then issued a declaration of independence on March 1, 1919, two days before the funeral of King Kojong. When he died in January, rumors spread that a Japanese physician had poisoned him, which provoked existing Korean hostility against Japan. The proclamation of independence gave the main impetus to a struggle for freedom among the entire Korean people.

The March First Movement quickly spread to the countryside, and more than one million people actively joined the mass parades, marching and police acted quickly to crush the March First Movement, killing hundreds of demonstrators and imprisoning thousands as well as burning villages and torturing civilians. Violent repression succeeded in eliminating all public vestiges of nationalism but alerted the world to Korea's plight. At Versailles, however, neither U.S. President Woodrow Wilson nor his counterparts did anything to challenge Japanese control over Korea.[58]

Japan's arbitrary but effective barriers against dissent compelled Koreans to work for outside assistance in pursuing independence for their nation. Korean patriots fled to China, the Soviet Union, and the United States, resulting in the unusual dominance of exiles in the Korean liberation movement. There was a profound absence of unity, however, as leaders came to

> shouting *"Taehan Toknip Manse"* (Long Live Korean Independence). Japan, stunned at the enormity of the movement, suppressed the peaceful demonstrations in March and April, killing more than 75,000, wounding more than 16,000, and arresting more than 46,000 Koreans.
>
> Although the March First Movement failed to win the support of either European powers or the United States, it awakened an independence-oriented Korean nationalism. Syngman Rhee, Kim Gu, Kim Kyu-sik, and other Korean leaders became members of the KPG established in Shanghai during April 1919. The KPG included both those who were already active overseas in lobbying for outside help to end Japanese colonialism and others who had fled into exile after Japan crushed the March First Movement. It failed, however, to enlist support from the United States, one of its primary goals. Despite the well-known antipathy of the Korean people to their Japanese overlords, Washington rebuffed the KPG's efforts for recognition during World War II because there were other contestants claiming the right to become Korea's government after liberation. The Korean nationalist uprising had attracted U.S. attention, however. Many American journalists reported on the March First Movement and denounced Japanese brutality in restoring control. In addition, some members of Congress criticized the U.S. government's pro-Japanese attitudes and expressed support for Korean independence.

advocate divergent ideologies, strategies, and values. The indifference of Western democracies at Versailles caused many Korean nationalists to seek support from the new Bolshevik government in Russia, which at that time was too weak to provide any material assistance. In September 1919, a diverse group of Korean politicians created the Korean Provisional Government (KPG) at a meeting in Shanghai, China. This group endorsed the constitution of the "Republic of Korea" that patriots had adopted the prior May in Seoul and confirmed election of Syngman Rhee, a student of Wilson's and a doctoral graduate of Princeton University, as its first president. Almost immediately, factual disputes made consensus impossible. After Kim Gu replaced him as president, Rhee opened a shadow legation in Washington, D.C., to promote his personal political aspirations. Meanwhile, Jiang Jieshi, leader of the Guomindang government at Nanjing, began providing financial support to the KPG in hopes of reasserting Chinese prerogatives in a liberated Korea.[59]

Challenging the KPG's claim to legitimacy were Koreans who favored both liberation and revolutionary changes in their country. These leftist leaders opposed the KPG because of its ties to the landowning and wealthy classes and rejected its emphasis on diplomacy and propaganda rather than direct action to halt Japanese rule. In this cohort was the Korean Communist Party, formed in 1921, which advocated a Bolshevik-inspired program to end poverty and oppression. Soviet leader Vladimir Lenin provided limited financial assistance and training for the Korean Communists, but in 1928 Moscow would withdraw its support because of factional disputes within the party. These Korean patriots continued to fight against Japanese colonialism, conducting guerrilla operations from bases in Siberia and Manchuria. They formed the Korean Independence League and recruited peasants in far northern Korea along the Yalu and Tumen rivers. In 1932, Kim Song-ju joined the partisans in China. Changing his name to Kim Il Sung, he won fame as a brave and resourceful fighter when he led a raid across the Yalu

River in 1937, seizing supplies, capturing hostages, and killing seven Japanese police.[60]

Resistance inside Korea went underground after the March First Rebellion. Japan pursued a course of escalating authoritarianism, exploiting Korea's human and economic resources to serve imperial interests. The colonial administration dissolved all political organizations, prohibited public assembly, denied free speech, censured and then closed newspapers, and banned the holding of firearms and other weapons. The Japanese dominated senior- and middle-level administrative positions at the provincial, town, and village levels but recruited Koreans for a police force. Agricultural productivity was the initial economic focus, with the application of modern techniques, irrigation, and fertilizer promoting a one-third increase in production from 1910 to 1930. Half of all rice was exported to Japan as Koreans experienced a 40 percent decrease in consumption and a steady decline in the standard of living.

In 1931, Japan shifted its emphasis to the promotion of industry and the development of hydroelectric power. A new Oriental Development Company supervised a vast array of internal improvements by constructing roads, railways, and harbor facilities; by managing land reclamation; and by providing electric, telegraph, and modern banking services. Japan also built hospitals and schools and improved sanitation and public health.[61]

Koreans hardly benefited from Japanese colonialism in other important respects, however. There was blatant discrimination in education. Mandatory elementary school attendance was a tactic to boost worker productivity, but half of all funds for education went to schools for children of the occupiers. Indoctrination in Japan's customs, along with instruction in the Japanese language, aimed at creating loyal imperial subjects. Policies for cultural regimentation included suppressing Korean traditions, outlawing the reading of Korean literature, restricting and then banning use of Hangul, and prohibiting teaching of Korean history. Military mobilization after Japan started a war with China in July 1937 only intensified these trends. Indeed, a virtual extinction of Korean identity seemed to be the ultimate objective. Edicts required Koreans to adopt Japanese-style names. Cities and towns received new Japanese names as well, as Seoul became Keijo and Pyongyang becoming Heijo. Korea simply disappeared behind the artificial boundary of Imperial Japan.[62]

Wartime economic mobilization in the Japanese Empire accelerated development in Korea. Specific projects included construction of a double-track rail bridge over the Yalu, the longest such structure in Asia at that time, and new plants for chemical and steel production, metal processing, and the manufacturing of machine tools. Japan relocated Korean peasants and laborers to Manchuria. During the 1930s, manufacturing production doubled to 40 percent of Korea's national output, whereas the number of individuals working in agriculture declined sharply. Hydroelectric power was the centerpiece of Japan's efforts, resulting in the building of massive facilities at Chosin and Fusen. The 3,000-foot-high Supung Dam, located 60 miles from Sinuiju—which had its powerhouse on the Korean side at Suiho—provided electricity for all of northern Korea and Manchuria. Japan's blueprint for establishing a self-sufficient "New Order" in East Asia placed Korea at the center of its hegemonic strategy. After U.S. entry into the Pacific war in December 1941, Japan imposed almost totalitarian control over Korea. Japan's policies sought complete integration of the peninsula into the imperial system and full mobilization of Korean manpower. Japan increased its occupation forces to 300,000 and reorganized the police before drafting Koreans for labor and military service.[63]

Imperial Japan's brutal treatment of Korea had an impact on Allied preparations for peace during World War II. In January 1943, the United States and Great Britain declared that the Allies would seek Japan's unconditional surrender to eliminate the possibility of its return to aggression. Another goal was the restoration of sovereignty to those nations that Japan had conquered in the construction of its empire. The Cairo Conference

During World War II, leaders of the Allied powers faced the issue of determining Korea's post-war government. Churchill, Truman, and Stalin met in August of 1945 at the Potsdam Conference, shown here, and failed to reach an agreement on Korea's postwar status.

late in 1943 was the most important wartime meeting about the future of Asia. U.S. President Franklin D. Roosevelt, British Prime Minister Winston Churchill, and China's Jiang Jieshi declared a commitment to fight for Japan's unconditional surrender and, with it, revocation of its special rights in China. They also discussed Korea, exposing a divergence of objectives among the Allies. China wanted to reassert dominance over the peninsula, whereas the United States favored Korean independence under a stable government that was the product of national self-determination. Because the Soviet Union was not yet at war with Japan, Premier Joseph Stalin was not at the Cairo Conference, but he made clear his desire for a "friendly" Korea that would not threaten Soviet interests in postwar Northeast Asia.[64]

Given that there had been prior Sino-Russian competition for control over the strategic peninsula, Roosevelt proposed a multinational, long-term trusteeship for Korea so that it would not reemerge as a source of conflict. His plan would provide protection and guidance for a liberated Korea before it gained future independence. This outcome also was preferable to the establishment of arbitrary borders that would divide the peninsula into spheres of influence. On December 1, 1943, Roosevelt, Churchill, and Jiang announced the signing of the Cairo Declaration, which stated that the three Allies, "mindful of the enslavement of the people of Korea, are determined that in due course Korea shall become free and independent." Korean nationalist leaders in exile reacted with anger and dismay to Allied plans to delay independence for Korea, insisting that they were fully capable of self-government. Rhee and others already were demanding that the United States recognize the KPG as Korea's legitimate postwar government. Ignoring this pressure, Roosevelt wanted to finalize the plan for a trusteeship at the Yalta Conference in February 1945. After Stalin supported this proposal, the two Allied leaders agreed to a four-power trusteeship plan to provide protection for Korea until it could maintain its own independence.[65]

Divisions within the Korean liberation movement provided compelling reasons against premature selection of a postwar Korean government. KPG President Kim Gu urged U.S. military assistance for the Korean Restoration Army, composed of 600 soldiers operating as an auxiliary unit under Jiang's military force. Another suitor for aid was the Sino-Korean Peoples' League, located in Manchuria. Finally, the Soviet Union was providing training and equipment to Korean guerrillas in Siberia, who were raiding Japanese installations in northern Korea. None of these groups had any governmental experience or demonstrable popular support inside Korea. Roosevelt therefore adopted a policy of impartiality toward all contestants for power in postwar Korea. In April 1945, however, Harry S. Truman became president after Roosevelt's death. At that time, Soviet expansion into Eastern Europe had begun to alarm U.S. leaders. Almost from the outset, the new president expected Soviet actions in Korea to parallel Stalin's policies in Eastern Europe, where the advancing Red Army was installing Communist governments. Less than one week after taking office, Truman reversed Roosevelt's position and abandoned support for trusteeships in liberated colonial areas.[66]

Visions of the replication in East Asia of the arbitrary boundaries that had been set in Eastern Europe separating democracy from communism dictated Truman's adoption of a policy that would lead to the exact same result. The new president was aware that the Soviet Union had not yet declared war on Japan, which provided the opportunity to remove any chance for Soviet expansion into Korea. Stalin continued to indicate his desire for a definitive Allied agreement on a Korean trusteeship because he anticipated that Koreans would greet Soviet forces as liberators. Moreover, Communists led the underground movement inside Korea, and there was mass support for radical reforms. Truman delayed making a firm settlement until the Potsdam Conference in July 1945, when he learned of U.S. success in testing of the atomic bomb. Japan's prompt surrender, he concluded, would preempt Soviet entry into the Pacific war, thereby permitting the United States to occupy Korea unilaterally and eliminate any possibility for sovietization. Truman's gamble failed, however. Two days after the U.S. atomic bomb attack on Hiroshima, Stalin declared war on Japan and sent the Soviet army into Korea. The closest U.S. troops were 600 miles away on Okinawa. Only Moscow's acceptance of Truman's eleventh-hour plan to arbitrarily divide Korea into Soviet and American zones of military occupation at the thirty-eighth parallel saved the peninsula from unification under Communist rule.[67]

Korea's division at the thirty-eight parallel established an illogical line that cut across natural areas of geographic, cultural, and climatic continuity. On the west coast, for example, a small peninsula was part of the U.S. zone, yet the United States possessed no land connection to that area. Significantly, the boundary was not entirely arbitrary because it separated two areas that were traditionally dissimilar. The north was rich in industry, hydroelectric power, and such minerals as coal, iron ore, and various chemicals. The south was more agricultural and produced large amounts of fish and rice but was also the center of textile and other light industries. Furthermore, the two zones possessed basic social and religious differences, as well as have been separated politically in ancient times. Divergent systems of land tenure represented yet another major contrast. Southern Korea suffered from both serious agrarian overpopulation and Japanese absentee landownership. The U.S. zone had an inordinate share of wealthy and conservative landlords, destitute farmer-tenants, and disgruntled workers. Landlordism was much less prevalent in the north, where plots were smaller and less productive. Circumstances thus existed from the start that would transform this unique arbitrary border into a permanent divide.[68]

Borders have drawn logic for their existence and acceptance from terrain features, ethnic differences, and historic tradition. None of these factors gave permanence to the choice of the thirty-eighth parallel in Korea. Great powers drew the line for reasons that related both to military expediency and to strategic competition. Koreans also had no voice in establishing this border and never accepted its legitimacy. The thirty-eighth parallel was perhaps the most arbitrary boundary in human history. It was also among the most unique. Borders separate people but rarely prevent economic, political, social, and cultural interaction. In Korea from 1945 to 1950, the thirty-eighth parallel was a nearly impenetrable barrier that precluded meaningful contact between two portions of the same population. Each group of Koreans would develop dramatically different plans for the future of a united country. Ironically, artificial division was responsible for the emergence of two authentic Koreas, which grew in strength with the subsequent formation of separate governments. Korea's example exposes how an arbitrary boundary can create circumstances resulting even in the permanent division of a homogeneous people in a historically united land.

5

A House Divided

Once Korea became a captive of the Cold War, its arbitrary division developed increasing durability. Wartime negotiations among the Allies suggested, however, that a Soviet-American deadlock on elimination of the division at the thirty-eighth parallel was far from inevitable. In fact, there were occasions between August 1945 and May 1948 when Washington and Moscow might have taken steps that could have resulted in Korea's peaceful reunification. In each case, however, international factors blocked agreement. Neither the United States nor the Soviet Union would accept a solution aimed at ending the partition because this might allow its adversary to dominate a reunited Korea. "The ultimate result of a great power rivalry," Callum MacDonald observed, "was to institutionalize [sic] the civil war in two contending states, both committed to the cause of unification."[69] A majority of Koreans tried but failed to prevent this outcome. Having created two Koreas, both the Americans and the Soviets provided each side with the means to wage war. Fierce nationalism drove Korean leaders in the north and the south to prepare to use force to reunite their nation. It was outside interference that created the arbitrary border dividing Korea and made possible the outbreak of a war to remove it.

President Harry S. Truman's refusal in the spring of 1945 to finalize terms of a trusteeship with the Soviet Union meant that there were no guidelines for coordination in the postwar administration of Korea. Worse still, ending the artificial division would require a diplomatic agreement. With Soviet-American relations experiencing a steady and serious deterioration in Europe, it was clear that neither Soviet leader Joseph Stalin nor Truman would want to compromise. U.S. forces arrived in southern Korea on September 8, 1945, nearly a month after Russian troops had entered the north. There to greet the Americans were representatives of the Korean People's Republic (KPR), an indigenous government that had won mass support among the Korean people because it advocated a sweeping reform program and had established a network of local committees. Lieutenant General John R. Hodge, the U.S. occupation commander, rejected the KPR's legitimacy, claiming that it was under Communist domination. Within a month, the United States faced agonizing problems in Korea. The Soviet occupation commander north of the thirty-eighth parallel refused to coordinate economic and administrative policy for uniformity in governing the two zones, and there had been little success in the south in controlling anti-imperialist agitation and revolutionary nationalism.[70]

By mid-September, the Truman administration realized that without a negotiated settlement, it had a painful choice: either prolonged occupation with permanent partitioning or withdrawal with Soviet domination of the entire peninsula. To escape this dilemma, it revived the trusteeship plan while continuing to hope that Moscow would agree to local coordination to implement uniform policies for occupation. During early October, however, the Soviet occupation commander was still spurning substantive negotiations. Faced with his intransigence, the United States asked Russia directly to authorize local negotiations for the coordination of occupation policy in Korea, removal of the partition at the thirty-eighth parallel, and the establishment of an international trusteeship. Positive steps toward the realization of Korean independence would include adequate and regular delivery of coal and electric power to the south, uniform fiscal policies, coast-wide shipping, orderly resettlement of displaced persons, and restoration of trade and communications between zones. When the Soviets did not respond, the United States decided to raise the issue of problems in Korea at the next Council of Foreign Ministers in December 1945.[71]

At the Moscow meeting, Secretary of State James F. Byrnes acted immediately to place the Korean matter on the agenda. The final U.S. proposal called for a trusteeship but focused instead on the vital necessity for local coordination to lift the barrier at the thirty-eighth parallel. After studying the U.S. proposal, Soviet Foreign Minister Vyacheslav Molotov accepted Byrnes's argument that local discussion of "urgent" questions was needed, but he wanted prior agreement on a long-term trusteeship plan. He satisfied this desire in his counterproposal, which contained four specific provisions. First, the major powers would establish a "provisional, democratic Korean government" to undertake all necessary measures for the development of Korean industry, transportation, agriculture, and culture. Second, representatives from Soviet and U.S. occupation forces would form a "joint commission," which would consult with local Korean parties and social organizations to formulate procedures to create a provisional government. Third, the joint commission would "work out measures of help and assistance (trusteeship) in the political, economic, and social progress" of Korea toward democratic self-government and independence. It also would formulate a five-year trusteeship plan and submit it for approval to the four major powers. Finally, the occupation commanders would convene a joint conference within two weeks to answer "urgent questions" and begin permanent coordination of administration.[72] This proposal held the promise of ending Korea's arbitrary border.

Byrnes approved Molotov's proposal after minor changes. Both the Soviet Union and the United States initially thought that the Moscow Agreement would lead to prompt reunification of Korea. News of the trusteeship plan, however, sparked a storm of angry protests in the U.S. zone that bordered on mass hysteria. Southern extremists held street demonstrations, closed stores and schools, and staged work stoppages. Rowdy youth groups roamed the streets of Seoul, intimidating U.S. military government personnel and distributing leaflets and posters decrying trusteeship. Conservative leader Kim Gu, who had returned from China in November 1945, organized an "Anti-Trusteeship Committee" in January 1946 dedicated to preventing implementation of the Moscow Agreement and restoring Korea's sovereignty as soon as possible. At first, Communists and those on the extreme left joined all Koreans in denouncing trusteeship, but they suddenly reversed direction and became the Moscow Agreement's most vocal defenders. During a demonstration on January 3, 1946,

The United Nations attempted to hold elections and help Korea establish an independent government after World War II, but the Soviet Union refused to grant the UN access to North Korea. The issue of reunification intensified in the late 1940s as it became clear that Stalin, seen here, was intent on pursuing the fight between communism and capitalism.

they hastily substituted the word "up" for "down" on their signs, which then read "Up with Trusteeship!"[73] Soviet officials may have ordered the switch, but the Communists certainly could not have expected the United States to endorse their political aspirations if they opposed trusteeship. More important, the extreme left understood that fulfilling the Moscow Agreement would remove the artificial border dividing Korea.

Soviet-American negotiations at the local level to answer "urgent questions" were an early test of the Moscow Agreement's chances for success. After 15 sessions, which began on January 16, 1946, it was clear that each side interpreted the accord differently. The Russians favored coordination of policy and the exchange of goods alone, whereas the Americans insisted on total administrative and economic integration. Nevertheless, the final Soviet-American agreement on administrative and economic coordination was an encouraging sign. Rail, truck, and coastal shipping trade between zones was resumed, as was nationwide mail service. Negotiators also agreed to create a permanent liaison between commands and to begin coordination at checkpoints along the parallel. Although the Soviets approved the use of uniform radio frequencies, they refused to permit free distribution of newspapers in the north or to allow unified fiscal policies. The Russians rejected joint control of transportation, electric power, and communications, arguing that a definitive arrangement would have to await the creation of a provisional government for all of Korea.[74] On balance, Soviet-American negotiations at the local level had made notable progress toward breaking down the artificial barrier dividing the Korean peninsula.

Soviet and American representatives met in Seoul on March 20, 1946, for the start of the joint commission negotiations. At first, Soviet chief delegate Terenti Shtykov resisted the American desire for nationwide consultations; he wanted discussion within each individual zone instead. Later, he favored consultation only with parties that backed the Moscow Agreement. The U.S. delegation responded that Korean hostility to the Moscow Agreement did not constitute an acceptable criterion for determining legitimacy, firmly resisting Moscow's attempt to exclude from consultation those parties belonging to the Anti-Trusteeship Committee.[75] Moscow's refusal to compromise on the issue was not surprising; it was exploiting the trusteeship issue as a device to prevent a sizable group of Korean leaders who were openly anti-Soviet from gaining access to postwar political power. Yet the United States was in the unenviable position of insisting on consultation with the very people who were bent on undermining the work of the joint commission. Fears of sovietization dictated the U.S. delegation's stand. The United States was certain that the exclusion of the conservatives would ensure a Communist seizure of power.

Soviet-American negotiations to implement the Moscow Agreement reached a deadlock when the U.S. delegation adamantly insisted on respect for absolute freedom of expression. On May 8, the joint commission adjourned, prompting predictions that this was the first step toward a civil war. Indeed, during the spring of 1946, rumors of armed clashes at the parallel increased, and scattered acts of violence were daily occurrences in the U.S. zone. Outside events closed what had seemed to be a promising road leading toward removal of the artificial border dividing Korea. The Soviets could have accepted consultation with Korean conservatives because left-wing leaders definitely would dominate the provisional government, even with right-wing participation. Early in 1946, however, Stalin publicly declared renewal of the worldwide struggle between communism and capitalism. Shortly thereafter, Winston Churchill, in his Iron Curtain speech, called on the United States to join Great Britain in defeating the Communist threat. Korea remained divided because the Cold War in Europe made Soviet-American cooperation impossible. Truman refused to surrender Korea to a Communist regime because this would damage U.S. credibility. He adopted a policy of delay, anticipating that the combination of patience and firmness would force Moscow to accept a plan for Korea's reunification on American terms.[76]

Soviet occupation officials north of the thirty-eighth parallel had already permitted the northern Koreans to elect representatives to local people's committees during the fall of 1945. When the United States yielded to southern protests against the Moscow Agreement, however, Moscow installed trusted clients in positions of authority. Kim Il Sung was the most important new leader in northern Korea; he arrived in the Soviet zone in

September 1945. In February 1946, he became chair of the "Provisional People's Committee." Moscow also satisfied the desires of most Koreans for sweeping social and economic change. In March 1946, in a major reform program, the northern Korean regime expropriated land belonging to Japanese collaborators, large landlords, and the church and redistributed this land without requiring cash payment. In June, it nationalized all major industries as well as transportation, communications, and

> **SYNGMAN RHEE (1875–1965)**
>
> Syngman Rhee was responsible for blocking the elimination of Korea's arbitrary boundary after World War II, because creating a separate government in the south would advance his personal political ambition. In August 1945, he became the first president of the ROK. Born in northern Korea, he studied the Chinese classics at home and then enrolled in an American Methodist school at Seoul in 1894. Rhee worked for antigovernment newspapers, leading in 1899 to his arrest and a life sentence in prison. His release came just before the Russo-Japanese War led to Japan's domination of Korea in 1905. King Kojong sent Rhee to see President Theodore Roosevelt in a failed appeal for help under the 1882 Treaty of Chemulpo. In 1907, he earned a Bachelor of Arts degree at George Washington University. Two years later, he received a Master of Arts degree from Harvard University and, in 1911, a doctorate in government at Princeton University. After the March First Rebellion in 1919, the KPG elected Rhee as its first president, although he was living in the United States. He established the Korean Commission in Washington, D.C., to lobby for recognition of the KPG, but he was impeached for misusing funds. Undaunted, Rhee went to Geneva in 1932 to lobby the League of Nations for mandate status for Korea to replace Japanese rule.
>
> After Japan's attack on Pearl Harbor in December 1941, Rhee delivered Voice of America broadcasts to Korea to incite an uprising against Japan. In February 1945, after the Yalta Conference, he openly argued that the Soviet Union would work to expand its influence in Asia, while criticizing its dominance over East Europe. When the United States and the Soviet Union divided Korea at the thirty-eighth parallel in August, Rhee falsely stated that, at Yalta, President Franklin D. Roosevelt had conceded to the Soviet demand for an

banking while mandating an eight-hour workday and proclaiming sexual equality.

These measures had a significant impact on the U.S. zone. Conservative members of the propertied classes fled south. In contrast to the Soviet Union, the United States delayed action on reform, waiting for the formation of a government to rule a reunited nation. Washington did, however, authorize elections for a South Korean Interim Legislative Assembly (SKILA) and

> ice-free port on the peninsula. His intense hostility toward the Soviet Union delayed his return to Korea as a "private citizen" until October. Conservatives, as well as the KPR, wanted him as their leader, but Rhee refused and began organizing his own party. An opponent of the Moscow Agreement for a Korean trusteeship, he went to the United States in 1946 to urge creating a separate southern government. Washington, for its own reasons, finally agreed. After UN-supervised elections established the ROK and his election as president, Rhee adopted a "March North" policy to reunify Korea, asking for military aid from Washington, which it refused to provide for fear of igniting a civil war.
>
> Rhee faced increasing opposition to his dictatorial rule and displeasure with economic deterioration, prompting North Korea to see itself as a liberator when it invaded the ROK in June 1950. Only U.S. troops kept Rhee in power. After the Inchon landing, he had his chance to rule a united nation with the removal of Korea's artificial border. China's entry ended this possibility, but Rhee pressed for continuing hostilities to achieve reunification. Thereafter, the United States twice considered initiating a coup to remove him, first when he imposed martial law in 1952 and later when he released North Korean prisoners of war in June 1953 to scuttle an armistice. Rhee survived, however, and bluffed the Eisenhower administration into agreeing in 1954 to a bilateral defense treaty in return for his promise not to obstruct the truce. Rhee's authoritarian rule intensified after the Korean War, exemplified in the passage of an unlawful constitutional revision in 1955 that allowed him unlimited terms of office. In 1956, he was elected president a third time. When the notorious rigged presidential election of March 1960 triggered the student uprising of April 19, 1960, however, it led to the ouster of Rhee, forcing him to resign and flee to Hawaii.

created a South Korean Interim Government (SKIG) to assume administrative responsibilities from the U.S. military government.[77] These events initiated a process that would eventuate in the creation of two Koreas.

Deadlock at the joint commission served the political interests of Syngman Rhee, who had returned to Korea in November 1945. If an arbitrary border continued to divide Korea, he thought that he could become president of a separate government in the south. The United States remained committed to reunification, however, and instructed occupation officials to sponsor Kim Kyu-sik and other political moderates for election to the SKILA. In October 1946, a violent mass uprising in response to widespread economic distress caused Hodge to fear a Communist seizure of power. Repression of the left allowed Rhee and other extreme conservatives to sweep the fraudulent SKILA elections.

U.S. officials were increasingly beginning to accept that artificial division was the only way to save a portion of Korea from Communist domination. The Soviet policy in the north early in 1947 was another reason for the United States to abandon further efforts to achieve early reunification. In November 1946, the Provisional People's Committee had held elections for representatives to create a permanent government. A "Congress of People's Committees" met in February 1947 and approved retroactively previous reforms. It also adopted a national economic plan to complete nationalization and to initiate agrarian collectivization. The congress created a permanent "People's Assembly," which elected a presidium to lead a separate regime in the north.[78]

Surprisingly, Washington and Moscow agreed to resume deliberations at the joint commission during May 1947. By this time, the Truman administration had adopted the containment policy to halt Soviet expansion in Europe, providing economic and military assistance to Greece and Turkey. Truman was prepared to apply the same approach in Korea and permanently divide the peninsula if the Soviets refused to accept U.S. terms. After two months of discussions, talks became deadlocked again over the issue of consultations. As planned, the Truman administration proposed economic aid to a separate government in South Korea, but Congress refused to fund the three-year program. In one final attempt to reunite the peninsula, Washington referred the Korean issue to the UN in September 1947. The following month, the United States submitted a resolution calling for the creation of UNTCOK to supervise free nationwide elections no later than March 31, 1948. In response, Moscow proposed an immediate end to the Soviet-American occupation of Korea to allow the Korean people to achieve reunification and independence. On November 14, the UN General Assembly passed the American-sponsored resolution by a wide margin.[79]

Many nations endorsed UN involvement in the Korean affair with reluctance, not least because the Soviet Union had opposed the resolution. Predictably, Hodge quickly pledged his full cooperation in the administration of UN-supervised elections in the U.S. zone, whereas the Soviet occupation commander ignored the UNTCOK. The United States pressed the UN to authorize elections only in the south. Events in the north confirmed that creating a separate South Korean government was an urgent necessity. In February 1948, the People's Committee announced its intention to form a government representing all of Korea within the next few months. In later statements, it condemned the UNTCOK as a tool of the United States and called on all southerners to resist the establishment of a separate government. The People's Committee also demanded immediate U.S. military withdrawal. Northern opposition to the UN resolution was understandable, given that it provided for a legislature with representation reflecting the south's two-to-one population superiority. Soviet cooperation was just as improbable because the close alignment of a large majority of UN members with the United States meant that the UN could not be fair and impartial. Also, Korea was the victim of escalating Cold War tensions after the Truman Doctrine and the Marshall Plan had placed the Soviets on the defensive.[80]

Some Korean leaders saw that if elections occurred only in southern Korea, this would make permanent the arbitrary border at the thirty-eighth parallel. Kim Kyu-sik, a respected moderate, joined with Kim Gu to cooperate with northern Koreans in arranging a North-South Conference to remove the partitioning of Korea. The Kims' campaign against separate elections in southern Korea, combined with mounting violence and disruption in the U.S. zone, contributed to UNTCOK's request for reconsideration of the UN decision to supervise elections if it had access only to southern Korea. The Truman administration, however, was determined to prevent any further delays, inaugurating a high-powered campaign to mobilize support in the UN for the U.S. position. In late February 1948, the UN Interim Committee authorized the supervision of elections in areas of Korea accessible to the UNTCOK. Washington's diplomatic pressure and the recent Communist coup in Czechoslovakia were the key factors in the Truman administration's triumph. Despite strenuous objections from some of its members, the UNTCOK voted to supervise the elections, thereby discarding the goal of reunification before or through a nationwide election. This decision meant that American occupation officials and right-wing politicians in southern Korea would be able to ignore moderate and left-wing demands for participation in the North-South Conference.[81]

Washington became virtually obsessed with preventing any further delays, scheduling the election for a Sunday. When several religious groups requested a one-day postponement, the United States refused. The administration grudgingly relented when it learned that a solar eclipse was expected on May 9 and Koreans would construe this as a bad omen. By this time, Washington had decided that a government under conservative domination in southern Korea would serve American interests. U.S. occupation officials permitted right-wing extremists to initiate a campaign of intimidation and violence against moderate and left-wing politicians, resulting in hundreds of deaths. On May 10, right-wing politicians and collaborators relied on police repression and outright terrorism to control an election that had only conservative candidates on the ballot. With moderates boycotting, the outcome was a resounding victory for the extreme right that hardly reflected the popular will. Nevertheless, the UNTCOK judged the results a "valid expression of the free will of the electorate in those parts of Korea which were accessible to the commission." Ominously, many victorious candidates, including Rhee, had been vocal in their campaign-related denunciations of Moscow for obstructionism and domination of the north.[82]

On May 31, 1948, South Korea's new legislative assembly formally convened in its opening session. Six weeks later, it promulgated a constitution and then elected Rhee as the first president. Formally established on August 15, the Republic of Korea (ROK) claimed to represent all of Korea, but the UN, acknowledging reality, conferred qualified recognition, declaring that it was the only legitimate government on the peninsula. Meanwhile, political developments in the north were moving along an identical path. In July, Kim Il Sung announced that a constitution for a national government with its capitol at Seoul was almost complete. On August 25, the People's Committee sponsored elections throughout Korea for delegates to a "Supreme Korean People's Assembly." Less than two weeks later, this body met in Pyongyang and promulgated the constitution. The assembly also elected a "Supreme People's Council" and chose Kim Du-bong as chair, who then selected Kim Il Sung as premier to head a cabinet that would be the ruling authority for the Democratic People's Republic of Korea (DPRK). This new government declared that it represented the entire nation and that it would send delegates to the UN.[83]

Two Koreas now menaced each other across an arbitrary boundary that replicated the Cold War line of hostility separating the United States and the Soviet Union around the globe. Because Koreans could not accept the thirty-eighth parallel as a legitimate border, war for reunification was only a matter of time. Outside interference in Korea's internal affairs had created this dangerous situation, and world events would continue to influence future developments on the peninsula. The Truman administration's application of the containment strategy in Korea, for example, sought to destabilize the Communist regime in the north. Evidence suggests that the DPRK decided to invade South Korea because it feared that this U.S. policy to achieve the collapse of communism in North Korea would ultimately succeed. Washington certainly did not hide its long-term expectation that the south would absorb the north. On August 15, 1948, South Koreans celebrated inauguration of the ROK and the formal end of U.S. military rule on the anniversary of Japan's surrender in World War II. At the ceremony, General Douglas MacArthur, the U.S. occupation commander in Japan, delivered a congratulatory speech. Korea's arbitrary border "must and will be torn down," he proclaimed. "Nothing shall prevent the ultimate unity of your people as free men of a free nation."[84]

6

Koreans Invade Korea

President Harry S. Truman never doubted that the Soviet Union ordered the North Korean military assault across the thirty-eighth parallel on June 25, 1950, as the first step in its plan to achieve global domination. Two days later, he declared that the Korean War "makes it plain beyond all doubt that the international Communist movement is prepared to use armed invasion to conquer independent nations."[85] "Communism," Truman stated later in his memoirs, "was acting in Korea just as Hitler, Mussolini, and the Japanese had acted ten, fifteen, and twenty years earlier." If this act of aggression were to go unchallenged, "the world was certain to be plunged into another world war."[86]

Although world politics were responsible for creating two Koreas, Truman's interpretation ignored the reality that internal factors explained the outbreak of the Korean War. North Korea invaded the south on June 25, 1950, for the purpose of eliminating the arbitrary boundary at the thirty-eighth parallel. If it had been stronger militarily, South Korea would have attacked first for the same reason. South and North Korea had adopted sharply contrasting political, social, and economic systems, reflecting the will of antagonistic occupiers. Motivating both Koreas was the same fierce nationalism that led to a brutal war causing millions of deaths and enormous destruction. After Soviet-American withdrawal, an artificial border could not restrain the determination of all Koreans to achieve reunification.

Syngman Rhee was obsessed with becoming the leader of a united Korea. When he became president of the ROK in August 1948, however, he knew that the DPRK was militarily superior to South Korea. North Korea had a large and well-trained army equipped with trucks, heavy artillery, and tanks. By contrast, the ROK's constabulary army had only light weapons. Incapable of halting an invasion from the north, the ROK government was petrified when the Soviet Union announced in September that its forces would withdraw before the year ended. Rhee instantly appealed to the Truman administration to delay removal of U.S. troops and increase South Korea's defensive capabilities.

U.S. military officials had insisted on withdrawal 90 days after the ROK's creation, ignoring State Department warnings that Communist seizure of control over all of Korea would damage U.S. global credibility.[87] Yet U.S. military withdrawal was indispensable to remove the appearance of dependence on the United States and to achieve international recognition of the ROK's legitimacy. In October 1948, a small group of Communists instigated a major rebellion at the southern tip of the peninsula. Soldiers, peasants, and workers joined the uprising, resulting in "people's courts" holding trials and ordering execution of thousands of policemen, military officers, and government officials. ROK forces restored order, but the rebellion shook the ROK's confidence and prompted a delay in U.S. withdrawal.[88]

During early 1949, the ROK seemed to be as artificial as the arbitrary border that divided the Korean peninsula. U.S. Ambassador John J. Muccio warned Washington that North Korea would invade and conquer South Korea that spring. In March, the Truman administration increased military assistance to the ROK and postponed complete military withdrawal until late June. It also continued its efforts to gain approval for a three-year economic aid program, as well as retaining diplomatic support from the UN. The United States had backed passage of a UN resolution the prior December providing for recognition of the ROK as the only legitimate government on the peninsula and sending a new commission to Korea to work for reunification. Washington hoped that application of containment in Korea would deter North Korea long enough to construct a strong and stable South Korea, providing hope for peaceful incorporation of the north at some future date. The Truman administration operated on the basic assumption that Moscow would respect the arbitrary boundary that it had established with Washington, control North Korea's leaders, and, with UN officials on the scene, prevent open military aggression.[89]

Kim Il Sung was just as determined as Rhee to reunite Korea under his own leadership, but he realized that the capacity of the United States to provide more assistance to the ROK than he could expect from the Soviet Union meant that time was not on his side. He therefore began to press Stalin for approval to attack South Korea within months after formation of the DPRK. Preparatory to an invasion, Kim Il Sung proposed the signing of a Soviet–North Korean Treaty of Friendship and Alliance in January 1949. Stalin flatly rejected the idea, arguing that it would receive world condemnation for perpetuating the artificial boundary dividing Korea. He no doubt also was avoiding an obligation to defend the DPRK if Kim started a war and the United States intervened. Starting early in 1949, Stalin became even more cautious in response to reports of military clashes at the thirty-eighth parallel. When Kim Il Sung headed a delegation that visited Moscow in March to secure expanded economic aid, Stalin made it clear that he would not sanction the DPRK's provoking a war in Korea. "The 38th parallel must be peaceful," he declared in a meeting with Kim. The North Korean leader still pressed for an invasion, telling Stalin that military means were needed to liberate all of Korea because "reactionary forces of the South will never agree on a peaceful reunification and will perpetuate the division of the country until they feel themselves strong enough to attack the North." It was the right moment to attack because the KPA was stronger than South Korea's army, guerrilla forces would support an invasion, and most southerners hated the Rhee regime.[90]

Once again, Stalin rejected Kim Il Sung's plea, explaining that the United States would view an attack as a violation of the agreement that had created Korea's artificial border and that the United States would intervene, thereby igniting a major war. He argued that an invasion was "not necessary" because South Korea would strike first and allow the DPRK to portray its offensive as a counterattack. Despite his warnings, Stalin's expectations of war in Korea rose after Kim Il Sung's departure. In April, Soviet Ambassador Terenti Shtykov reported from Pyongyang that the United States was supporting a military buildup in the south. More alarming, the ROK was moving troops to the parallel in accordance with plans for an invasion and had already crushed guerrilla forces in South Korea. Shtykov predicted an attack in June.

These dire warnings of North Korea's vulnerability reinforced Kim Il Sung's determination to gain not only Soviet approval for forcible reunification but also the military assistance needed to achieve this objective. In April 1949, he proposed to Stalin the immediate expansion of the DPRK's mechanized and airpower capacities.[91] Subsequent U.S. efforts to strengthen the ROK placed pressure on Moscow to satisfy Kim's request. In June 1949, the State Department asked Congress for $150 million in economic aid for the ROK. U.S. troops withdrew from South Korea later that same month, but in July, as part of a larger bill, Congress allocated $10.9 million in military aid for South Korea.[92]

Kim Il Sung had already decided that he could not depend entirely on a reluctant Stalin. In early May 1949, he had approached the Chinese Communists, hoping that they would back his invasion plans. Mao Zedong approved of Pyongyang's desire to liberate the south and even promised assistance from Chinese troops if necessary. He advised against haste, however, urging that the DPRK not attack South Korea in the "near future" because world conditions were unfavorable and China was preoccupied with its civil war. In anticipation of victory, Mao confirmed plans to return two divisions of Korean troops fighting in China. Pyongyang's pressure on the Chinese to support a military assault on the ROK increased Soviet anxiety about the imminence of war in Korea. Stalin faced a difficult dilemma. It was vital to provide the DPRK with enough military aid to deter an attack from the south without giving so much that Kim Il Sung could initiate an invasion. In June 1949, Moscow and Pyongyang signed a protocol on military-technical assistance, providing for the Soviet Union to supply its ally with large amounts of combat aircraft, tanks, cannon, landing ships, machine guns, and engineering equipment. Stalin would not approve an invasion, however, because he believed that North Korea had not achieved either military superiority north of the parallel or political strength south of that line.[93]

During the summer of 1949, Stalin's concerns about South Korea's threat to the survival of North Korea increased in response to the escalating intensity of military clashes at the arbitrary boundary dividing the peninsula. Battalion-sized and larger units often were involved, and casualties were heavy. Both sides initiated the engagements, with opposing forces at times penetrating miles into the other's territory. Carefully orchestrated, these battles sought to drive home political points, gather intelligence, and keep the enemy off balance. ROK forces began

> ### KIM IL SUNG (1912–1994)
> Kim Il Sung was the first premier of the DPRK and initiated the Korean War to eliminate the arbitrary boundary dividing the peninsular nation at the thirty-eighth parallel. Born Kim Song-ju to a peasant family near Pyongyang, he later assumed the name of a legendary guerrilla fighter and became a well-known anti-Japanese guerrilla commander. During World War II, the Soviet Union organized the "Operating Group in Korea," along with the Korean guerrilla leaders in its eighty-eighth division, and named Division Captain Kim Il Sung as its leader. In September 1945, he returned to Korea and subsequently used both his guerrilla record and the support of Soviet occupation authorities to become the leader of North Korea. Kim Il Sung had a burning ambition to reunite his country and, with Soviet and Chinese acquiescence and support, invaded the ROK on June 25, 1950. Victory seemed near when the forces of the ROK and the United States along with 15 other nations under the flag of the UN repulsed the assault. Massive Chinese intervention in the Korean War saved the North Koreans from defeat and the DPRK from destruction.
>
> After the Korean War, Kim Il Sung systematically eliminated his political rivals, among them Pak Hon-yong, leader of the anti-Japanese underground movement in Korea during World War II. He then created a highly centralized system that accorded him unlimited power and generated a formidable cult of personality. His subjects eventually revered him as their *suryong*, or "Great Leader." He used the *juche*, or self-reliance ideology, to legitimize his regime. Under his rule, the DPRK became isolated from the world community and hard-pressed economically. In particular, after his death, North Korea became

posturing along the parallel in the spring as American troops withdrew. Rhee publicly advocated forcible reunification and turned ROK commanders loose, resulting in serious fighting at Kaesong and on the isolated Ongjin Peninsula to the west. The DPRK at first allowed the ROK to gain local superiority because it controlled the border with lightly armed border guards and held its army in reserve. Later, North Korea committed its regular troops and pummeled South Korean forces to silence Rhee's talk of "March North." Both Koreas staged other incidents to

> increasingly unable to stabilize its sinking economy and feed its people. Kim died of a heart attack just before a historic summit with ROK President Kim Young-sam, set for July 1994. Kim Jong Il, his son, then made a dynastic succession. Kim Il Sung was as omnipresent in death as in life, and the junior Kim ruled the DPRK in accordance with the teachings of the departed "Great Leader" as the nation's "Dear Leader."
>
> Kim Il Sung had made the United States his and the DPRK's number one enemy, blaming Washington for dividing Korea with an artificial border in 1945, intervening in 1950 to block reunification on his terms, and turning South Korea into its colony. Thus, he had pursued a hostile policy toward the United States, as shown in the U.S.S. *Pueblo* seizure in 1968 and the axe murders in 1976 of two American military officers in the DMZ. On the other hand, Kim Il Sung had long sought to make contact with the United States in hopes of persuading Americans to withdraw from the peninsula. He also hoped that the beginning of a relationship with Washington could substitute for a collapse of the DPRK alliance with the Soviet Union and the weakening of its relations with the PRC. After March 1993, he used North Korea's nuclear weapons program as a bargaining chip to trade for recognition, security assurances, and economic benefits from the United States. For a dilapidated and isolated regime with few other cards to play, the brinkmanship strategy was surprisingly successful. When Kim Il Sung died, the U.S. government expressed its condolence to Pyongyang, which shocked the ROK government and many South Koreans. The survival of the DPRK stands as a tribute to the life of a remarkable politician with an unmatched instinct for survival.

cover the infiltration of guerrillas, usually Communist partisans but at times ROK irregulars.[94]

North Korea started its share of border clashes but concentrated more on building a revolutionary base for guerrilla operations in the ROK. As the military balance tilted in its favor as a result of Soviet arms deliveries, Pyongyang launched a concerted campaign against southern "invasions" of its territory. In heavy fighting at Ongjin, Kaesong, and Chunchon, the KPA drove ROK forces from salients (military positions that project into the position of the enemy) north of the parallel. The campaign included a huge Liberation Day parade to display its newly acquired weaponry, a "show" trial for captured ROK guerrillas, and a fund-raising drive to buy more Soviet tanks and planes. It ended with Foreign Minister Pak Hon-yong sending a warning to the UN that if it continued to interfere on the Korean peninsula, the Korean people would have to rely on their own means to unify the country. Except for a brief clash on Ongjin, there were few major border incidents after this until the start of the Korean War. ROK commanders adopted a much lower stance along the parallel, avoiding fights that they could no longer win. Nonetheless, military action after Rhee's calls to "March North "created fears about his plans to ignite a war and led Washington to limit the military capabilities of the ROK. Rejecting requests for airplanes and naval vessels, the United States also refused to provide tanks or heavy artillery. Most important, the border clashes confirmed the ROK's threat to the DPRK, bolstering Kim Il Sung's case to Stalin for approval of an invasion.[95]

For the remainder of 1949, Moscow continued to reject Pyongyang's requests for approval of its plan to stage even a limited invasion because a quick victory was unlikely. The establishment of the People's Republic of China (PRC) in October, however, had a decisive impact on events in Korea. Mao's victory in China motivated Kim Il Sung to increase his pressure on Stalin, telling Shtykov that it meant Korea "was next in line." Kim asked to visit Moscow to plead his case, and the Soviet leader agreed, advising Shtykov, "I am prepared to help him in this matter."[96]

Kim Il Sung and Pak Hon-yong spent almost all of April in Moscow. In the first of three meetings, Stalin explained that the "international environment has sufficiently changed to permit a more active stance on the unification of Korea."[97] He believed that the Soviet testing of an atomic bomb in September 1949 and the signing of the Sino-Soviet Treaty of Friendship and Alliance would make the United States much "more hesitant to challenge the Communists in Asia." Stalin told Kim, however, that he could launch an offensive only if the PRC approved. Kim Il Sung replied that a military victory would be easy, especially because of support from the guerrilla movement in the south and an expected mass uprising against the Rhee regime. Having secured Stalin's conditional approval, the North Korean leader traveled to Beijing and met with Mao on May 15. After Kim alleged that Stalin had approved his plans, Mao gave his reluctant consent for the offensive as well.[98] Kim Il Sung had deftly manipulated his patrons into supporting his desperate bid for reunification before Rhee could beat him to the punch.

Koreans considered proposals for peaceful reunification just prior to the start of the Korean War. On June 7, the Democratic Front for the Unification of the Fatherland (DFUF) called for nationwide elections in early August to elect a unified assembly that would convene in Seoul on August 15, the fifth anniversary of liberation. To prepare for these elections, Pyongyang proposed that a joint conference of political leaders from both sides of Korea's arbitrary border meet at Haeju or Kaesong in the middle of June. As a condition of northern participation, the DFUF demanded exclusion of Rhee, other right-wing politicians, and the UN. When three northerners crossed the parallel to deliver the proposal, ROK guards promptly placed them in custody. Pyongyang then offered to exchange Cho Man-sik, a prominent Christian nationalist, for two imprisoned southern Communist leaders, but Rhee attached unacceptable conditions that prevented the swap. The DPRK floated another unification initiative on June 19 proposing the merger of its Supreme People's Assembly and the South Korean legislature. A possible eleventh-

KOREA DIVIDED

In this photograph, North Korean refugees climb a shattered bridge across the Taedong River as they flee from advancing Chinese Communist troops. China entered the war, which was fought to unify Korea, as allies of North Korea, in October, 1950.

hour attempt to find an alternative to war, the proposal may have sought to determine whether new anti-Rhee assemblymen who had gained election the prior month were more open to reconciliation. Finally, in showing that its own intentions were peaceful, the DPRK was building a case to justify its resorting to war and to mobilize the populace to fight it.[99]

Early on the morning of June 25, 1950, DPRK forces crashed across the artificial boundary dividing Korea. The KPA was composed of about 135,000 well-trained troops, including 38,000 Koreans recently returned from fighting in China. Armed with tanks and artillery, the North Koreans sent the weaker and smaller ROK army into a helter-skelter retreat. With the approval of the UN, the United States committed four combat divisions to save the ROK but could not halt the KPA advance until the middle of August, when a defensible front stabilized along a rectangular perimeter around the southeastern port of Pusan.[100] By then, the DPRK had possessed administrative control over most of the ROK for nearly two months. While the KPA attempted to overrun the Pusan Perimeter, thousands of northern and southern Korean Communists worked to reshape the political, social, and economic structure south of a former arbitrary border. The first objective was to reestablish the people's committees that the American military government had disbanded during the first two years of U.S. occupation. Throughout the period of the KPA occupation, DPRK propaganda in the south emphasized consistently the democratic and popular nature of the committee form of government, contrasting it with what the DPRK labeled the "ruling organs of Japanese imperialism."[101]

Many southerners greeted the KPA as an army of liberation, believing that the United States had imposed a colonial state on the south and welcoming an end to Rhee's regime. During the retreat southward, Rhee had ordered execution of 50,000 political prisoners, and the KPA uncovered mass graves at Taejon revealing one particularly brutal atrocity. A large majority of the workers and half the students in Seoul rallied behind the DPRK, many voluntarily enlisting in the KPA. In late July, nearly 50 members of the ROK National Assembly who had remained in Seoul after the war began held a meeting and declared their allegiance to the DPRK. South Korean Communists exploited this popular support to form a Seoul people's committee, which quickly confiscated property belonging to the ROK government, its officials, and "monopoly capitalists." The KPA distributed surplus rice to the poor, and Communist cadres prepared for radical land redistribution. The DPRK also released political prisoners, many of whom assumed responsibility for administering local justice. Not surprisingly, a reign of terror followed, as those recently imprisoned gained retribution from their former oppressors. Elsewhere in the ROK, however, the reemergence of local people's committees was less spontaneous. The DPRK cadres ensured that the membership conformed to the DPRK's practice and discipline.[102]

Unfulfilled expectations of widespread uprisings in support of the DPRK created overconfidence, which contributed to delays in the KPA's advance southward. Pyongyang sent two of its best divisions into the southwestern Cholla provinces, where Communist support was strongest, to recruit additional troops. By late August, the United States was superior to the KPA in numbers and equipment and held air control. During September, the North Koreans could not build on breaks in the Pusan Perimeter because of shortages of food, ammunition, and fuel as well as reliance on young and inexperienced conscripts. Declining morale was rampant in an exhausted North Korean army.

On September 15, a U.S. amphibious landing at the west coast port of Inchon reversed the course of the war. U.S. forces broke out of the Pusan Perimeter, and the KPA fled northward. Liberation of Seoul on September 28 ended Kim Il Sung's bid to reunite Korea. Previously, the DPRK had not condoned a policy of terror, but now there were large-scale massacres. When ROK officials regained control in South Korea, a new round of violent and bloody retribution punished collaborators with North Korea. More important, Rhee now could act on Kim Il Sung's elimination of Korea's arbitrary border and impose authority over a united nation. On September 30, ROK forces crossed the parallel in pursuit of forcible reunification.[103]

For nearly two months, Rhee's government worked to complete imposition of its authority on North Korea. On October 10, the ROK's home minister announced that the national police controlled nine towns north of the parallel, with a special force of 30,000 being recruited for occupation duty. Two days later, the UN announced that it would recognize no government as having "legal and effective control" over all of Korea. Ignoring international objections to Rhee's regime, roughly 2,000 national police crossed Korea's now nonexistent arbitrary boundary. In Pyongyang, the notorious "Tiger" Kim Chong-won, known for his brutal treatment of suspected Communists, was in charge, and right-wing youth groups held political indoctrination sessions. Some writers claimed that as part of this right-wing counterrevolution, the ROK, as a matter of official policy, sought to locate and destroy Communists and collaborators. The DPRK later reported that Rhee's agents executed "hundreds of thousands" of North Koreans. Despite world protests, the Truman administration was not entirely displeased with the extension of ROK authority northward. Early in November, it instructed U.S. military authorities in the north that it "is not intended that pertinent directives ... prohibit the use of ROK administrators, police, military forces, or any other ROK asset in North Korea ...."[104] Because South Korean agents were loyal to Rhee, the UN would have had trouble reversing the trend had the issue not become moot with Chinese military intervention.[105]

On November 25, China's "People's Volunteers" launched a counteroffensive to prevent the destruction of the DPRK. As U.S. forces retreated southward, reimposition of Communist rule on North Korea was very unpleasant. Distrustful of the loyalty of the people, the DPRK executed, imprisoned, or ostracized countless individuals in areas that the ROK's officials had occupied. Kim Il Sung, however, would not achieve a complete restoration of power until the armistice ended fighting in July 1953, because the Chinese were in charge in North Korea. This reality provides an example of how outside powers played a central role in the origins, conduct, and outcome of the Korean War. "A shrimp is crushed in the battle of whales," one Korean proverb fittingly laments.[106] In truth, it was Koreans who initiated the three-year war that would ravage their nation. An intense nationalism made it impossible for those living on either side of the thirty-eighth parallel to tolerate the artificial border dividing the peninsula. Governments representing sharply contrasting visions of the appropriate social, economic, and political system for a united nation reflected the larger Soviet-American Cold War contest for global power and added intensity to the military clash. This was a war fought to eliminate an arbitrary border, however, underlining the reality that this conflict was by name and nature Korean.

7

Partition for Peace

Koreans waged a kind of war along the thirty-eighth parallel almost from the moment that it was established by Soviet-American agreement as an arbitrary boundary in 1945. On June 25, 1950, this conflict entered its conventional phase when Premier Kim Il Sung of the DPRK ordered an offensive southward to reunite his country. President Syngman Rhee of the ROK agreed with his adversary in the north that the artificial border dividing Korea had no legitimacy. On July 13, Rhee declared that the Communist invasion had obliterated the line allegedly separating two Koreas. On June 29, however, U.S. Secretary of State Dean Acheson had disagreed. He insisted that military action "is solely for the purpose of restoring the [ROK] to its status prior to the invasion from the north and reestablishing the peace broken by aggression."[107] By August, however, the Truman administration had decided to seek forcible reunification. Chinese intervention in November 1950 forced the United States to return to Acheson's original definition of its war aims. After U.S. forces scored major battlefield victories in the spring of 1951, China was ready to accept restoration of the prewar status quo. This created the need for a new line dividing Korea, but not at the thirty-eighth parallel. The armistice negotiations would lead to creation of a DMZ across the peninsula. This arbitrary boundary still separates two Koreas at the start of the twenty-first century.

China's entry into the Korean War dramatically altered Kim Il Sung's thinking about the line dividing the Korean peninsula. This was because the PRC had decided to intervene only with great reluctance. Once the United States had committed troops, Beijing was certain that the DPRK would fail to conquer South Korea. In July, it began to warn Pyongyang that the United States would land at Inchon and pummel a retreating KPA. Once this prediction became reality, the Chinese watched with increasing unease as U.S. forces advanced to the Yalu River. Joseph Stalin was unwilling to send Soviet troops to Korea and ignite a world war. He therefore pressed the PRC to intervene to save the DPRK, but Mao Zedong refused because the Soviet leader would not pledge air support. Early in October, both Moscow and Beijing were ready to allow the United States to destroy the DPRK, fearing the consequences of a more widespread war. Mao finally decided to intervene after learning of Stalin's expectation that the PRC would allow Kim Il Sung to set up a government in exile in Manchuria.[108]

Betrayal at the hands of his Communist patrons had a powerful and indelible impact on Kim Il Sung. Near-destruction of the DPRK in the fall of 1950 caused him to lose faith in protection from the Soviet Union and China, leading to his later transformation of North Korea into an isolated and totalitarian state capable of defending itself against U.S. imperialism.

Kim Il Sung recognized that Chinese intervention once again had made conquest of the south possible but that the reunited Korea that emerged might not be under his control. By January 1951, Chinese forces had pushed U.S. forces into South Korea. The DPRK occupied the northern half of the ROK, but the Chinese People's Volunteers Army was in charge. This second occupation also was too brief for implementation of well-conceived or long-range programs. More important, U.S. forces regrouped under the inspirational leadership of a new commander, General Matthew B. Ridgway. By the end of February, a series of counteroffensives had pushed the Chinese north of the thirty-eighth parallel. President Truman then decided to propose a cease-fire as prelude to negotiations for an armistice, but UN Commander General Douglas MacArthur scuttled this peace initiative. Without the president's approval, he issued a public ultimatum on March 24 demanding an immediate meeting with the enemy commander to discuss terms for a cease-fire and steps to achieve reunification. Rejection, he warned, would mean that Chinese forces would face utter destruction, with retaliatory attacks likely extending beyond Korea. Five days later, Radio Beijing defiantly rejected what sounded like a demand for surrender. On April 11, Truman recalled MacArthur in response to this latest act of insubordination.[109]

Beijing, unlike Washington, remained determined to reunite

China, under the leadership of Mao Zedong, intervened in the Korean War with extreme reluctance. Like his ally Stalin in the Soviet Union, Mao, seen here, was afraid of igniting a world war, but as the U.S. advanced he relented and sent troops in late 1950.

Korea. During April and May 1951, the Chinese launched two massive offensives aimed at destroying enemy forces and pushing the United States out of Korea. UN ground troops stood firm against enemy night attacks and human wave tactics, while artillery and air attacks inflicted huge casualties on Chinese and

North Korean forces. Counterattacks then moved battle lines almost 20 miles above the thirty-eighth parallel. By June, the PRC recognized that it could not win a battlefield victory in Korea, accepting the necessity of an armistice that would restore an arbitrary boundary to divide the peninsula. Meanwhile, a U.S. Senate joint committee was conducting hearings to investigate Truman's reasons for firing MacArthur. These deliberations would have importance for the future of Korea because U.S. officials specifically referred to the thirty-eighth parallel as being suitable for an armistice line. Truman and other top U.S. officials had made public references to the parallel as an acceptable border separating the two Koreas after a cease-fire. General Omar N. Bradley implied as much when he testified that implementation of MacArthur's plan for victory would lead to the "wrong war, in the wrong place, at the wrong time, and with the wrong enemy."[110]

At first, U.S. military leaders also provided indirect support for restoration of the old line. On May 31, 1951, the Joint Chiefs of Staff (JCS) dispatched new instructions for General Ridgway, who had replaced MacArthur as UN commander, regarding future prosecution of the war that for the most part would remain in effect until the war ended. Ridgway was to continue to "inflict maximum personnel and materiel losses" on enemy forces "within the geographic boundaries of Korea," but the new aim was "to create conditions favorable to a settlement of the Korean conflict."[111] This goal envisioned an enforceable cease-fire that guaranteed the administrative authority and military defense of the ROK south of a boundary line at least as far north as the thirty-eighth parallel. There would be provisions for the gradual withdrawal of all non-Korean armed forces coupled with the buildup of sufficient ROK military power to deter or repel a renewal of North Korean aggression. On June 30, the ROK issued a formal announcement opposing an armistice and insisting on reunification. Condemning any limitation on its sovereignty, it demanded withdrawal of Chinese troops, disarmament of the North Korean army, and participation in all future conferences about Korea. Rhee orchestrated large public demonstrations thereafter to place pressure on the United States to resume the offensive into North Korea.[112]

Late in May 1951, the United States had approached the Soviet Union indirectly to determine its position on an armistice in Korea. Stalin did not share this information with the Chinese but told Beijing that an "armistice is now advantageous." He agreed to send military advisors if needed as well as arms for 16 divisions, and nine divisions of jet warplanes. Beijing and Pyongyang should expect a U.S. proposal for armistice negotiations, Stalin divulged, but wanted a ground assault before then and preparations to hold a new front. Mao replied on June 13 that Communist forces were too weak because of the spring offensives to comply at that time and "must occupy a defensive position for the next two months." He then stated that China's objectives at the talks would be

> restoration of the border at the 38th parallel; to apportion from both North Korea and South Korea an insignificant strip [to serve] as a neutral zone. A proposal that the neutral zone come only from the territory of North Korea will by no means be accepted. North and South Korea [should not] interfere with one another.

Mao would begin plans for an offensive in August if the United States did not stage an assault behind Communist lines. One week later, he reiterated his requests for additional artillery, tanks, rifles, planes, vehicles, and spare parts, complaining that a disparity in equipment with the enemy had existed since China had first intervened.[113]

On June 23, 1951, when Soviet UN Ambassador Jacob A. Malik suggested in a radio speech that the two sides should seek a cease-fire, Moscow complied with Mao's desire for a Soviet reply to the U.S. initiative. Ridgway's proposal on June 30 to begin truce talks aboard a Danish hospital ship in Wonsan Harbor was welcome news for China and North Korea. Stalin had already conveyed approval to Mao for an arrangement that the Soviets had worked out with the U.S. ambassador in Moscow, which provided for each side to have two delegates representing military units rather than governments. In response, Mao ordered General Peng Dehuai, China's commander in Korea, and Kim Il Sung to prepare to send representatives immediately. His fears of a new U.S. amphibious landing caused Mao to oppose Wonsan Harbor as a negotiating site. He warned Stalin that it was a prime target because it was "a fortified sea base of North Korea." As an alternative, the Communists demanded a meeting in Kaesong. Choice of this city, located just north of the thirty-eighth parallel, symbolized the expectation that an arbitrary boundary again would divide Korea. The United States, expecting swift progress toward an armistice, accepted Kaesong as a meeting site in part because it was then unoccupied by either side. When the talks began, however, Communist forces had moved into the ancient capital, ensuring Communist control over the conference site.[114]

Rhee refused to sanction the negotiations at Kaesong, although eventually he sent an observer. By contrast, Kim Il Sung supported the PRC's pursuit of an armistice. To be sure, he was dependent on Beijing as well as Moscow for the economic and military support vital to his government's survival, just as Rhee relied on the Americans. He was less certain of the Chinese and Soviet commitment to the DPRK's survival than was Rhee regarding the support of the United States. North Korea, however, unlike the south, was suffering tremendous damage from aerial bombardment. Reflecting North Korea's desire for peace, General Nam Il, the KPA's chief of staff, was named the chief Communist delegate, although Beijing set policy. Nam's counterpart was U.S. Vice Admiral C. Turner Joy.

Acrimony surrounded the first negotiating sessions at Kaesong. Communist photographers greeted the UN delegation's arrival in vehicles that displayed white flags. Competition followed to see who had the biggest flag and the highest seats. The Communists refused to allow UN news reporters at Kaesong until Ridgway made their presence a condition for more talks.[115] Agreement on an agenda was the first item for substantive discussion. The negotiators proposed conflicting drafts but resolved this issue rather easily after just two weeks of honest bargaining. Both sides at first anticipated swift agreement on an armistice.

Debate over the agenda identified the issue of Korea's future arbitrary boundary as an immediate source of contention. Disagreement focused not only on whether the withdrawal of foreign troops from Korea would be a precondition for negotiations but also on whether the thirty-eighth parallel would be a line of demarcation for a cease-fire. On July 16, Joy presented a revised United Nations Command (UNC) agenda proposal that had four points:

1. Adoption of agenda
2. Establishment of a DMZ as a basic condition for the cessation of hostilities in Korea
3. Formation of concrete arrangements for a cease-fire and armistice
4. Creation of arrangements relating to prisoners of war (POWs)

The U.S. position was that the Communist desire to include provisions for withdrawal of foreign troops was not one to be negotiated in the field, but Washington hinted that the issue would pose no problem if the other side were sincere in its pursuit of an armistice in Korea. Showing their desire for an agreement, the Communists proposed adding a fifth agenda item calling for a postarmistice conference to negotiate the withdrawal issue. On July 26, the two sides formally adopted a bilateral draft of a five-item agenda.[116] The brief clash over the agenda signaled that agreement on a postwar artificial border for Korea would be a major issue testing the desire of the combatants for an early armistice.

Setting aside the issue of POW repatriation, the negotiators might have achieved an armistice agreement in just four months had the United States not chosen to advance a preposterous proposal to resolve agenda item two. Nam Il reacted with understandable anger when the UNC, seeking a propaganda victory, arbitrarily proposed a border deep in North Korea. He ridiculed the claim "that the advantages we would gain by the cessation of Air and Naval attacks by the UN forces would be greater than the advantages given up by us in the withdrawal by our ground forces to the line running through Pyongyang and Wonsan."[117] The UNC made it impossible for the Communists even to consider its proposal that the line of battle be a demarcation line because this would imply acceptance of military inferiority. Accusing the UNC of arrogance and a lack of good faith, Nam Il adopted an inflexible stand demanding the thirty-eighth parallel as the armistice line. On August 10, the UNC delegation indicated its willingness to discuss a DMZ based on the existing line of ground contact, but the Communists refused. There followed a "period of silence, lasting two hours and eleven minutes."[118]

For the United States, the thirty-eighth parallel was unacceptable for two reasons. First, U.S. military leaders viewed the line as both artificial and difficult to defend. They opposed the abandonment of the fortified front occupied by the UNC north of the parallel, except for a short section stretching from Kaesong west to the coast. Second, ending the war north of the prewar boundary would provide physical proof of the defeat of North Korea's aggression. Naturally, the Communists assigned great symbolic value to restoring the thirty-eighth parallel as evidence of their victory in preventing the UNC from conquering North Korea. After two weeks of haggling, the Chinese faced a difficult dilemma. The UNC would not accept the thirty-eighth parallel as a cease-fire line, but Beijing considered acceptance of a buffer zone on the basis of the battlefront a sign of weakness. The PRC was not prepared to undertake another costly offensive. Its only alternative was to terminate talks over the issue. Beijing halted the negotiations unilaterally at the meeting on August 23, 1951, charging that an alleged UNC air attack based on fabricated evidence near Kaesong meant that the conference site was not safe.[119]

Soldiers in Korea, on all sides, faced harsh conditions during a frustrating war in which battles were often fought just to push the opposition across the 38th Parallel, not for victory. Here, U.S. Marines brace against frigid cold and snow in North Korea's Chosin Reservoir region.

A willingness to wait also existed inside the Truman administration. Just before suspension of talks, the UNC delegation had received instructions to repeat its rejection of the thirty-eighth parallel and to continue the talks with "calmness, firmness, and patience" until the Communists altered their stand. The UNC escalated the ground war and after heavy fighting moved the battle line further north. The United States also dropped dummy atomic bombs on North Korea to intimidate the DPRK. Then, on September 10, a U.S. plane strafed Kaesong in error, providing a pretext for the Communist delegation to justify its prior claims that the area was not safe. Satisfied with the UNC's immediate apology, the Communists signaled a willingness to resume talks. Truce negotiations remained suspended for six more weeks because Ridgway insisted on moving the conference site. On October 7, Nam Il yielded to the UNC's demand to resume talks at Panmunjom, a village about six miles east of Kaesong. When talks resumed on October 25, the Communists abandoned their insistence on the thirty-eighth parallel but proposed a demarcation line that required the UNC to surrender most of its holdings above that line. The UNC delegation flatly rejected the proposal.[120]

Ridgway began to oppose a permanent truce line, arguing that this would preclude the use of ground offensives to hasten a final agreement if the enemy refused to compromise on other issues. The Truman administration wanted to avoid charges that it was slowing progress toward peace, fearing that this would jeopardize support among its allies for action at the UN. On November 13, the JCS instructed Ridgway to settle the issue immediately based on the line of contact, suggesting that this be effective for a period of one month. Four days later, the UNC delegation, despite Ridgway's strong protest, proposed a DMZ four kilometers wide at the current battle line. If the sides could not sign an armistice within 30 days, subsequent combat would result in revision of the line.[121]

Pyongyang placed pressure on Beijing and Moscow to accept, issuing an appeal to the UN for action to speed progress toward "immediate cessation of military operations in Korea ... the withdrawal of troops along the front line and the creation of a two kilometer demilitarization zone."[122] On November 27, after locating a specific line of contact, both sides agreed that a provisional demarcation line would become the final one if they signed the armistice within 30 days. Neither side questioned the agreement after the grace period ended, resulting in this provisional line's becoming a de facto demarcation line and the basis for the DMZ at the last stage of the fighting.[123]

On the same day that the negotiators agreed on a provisional demarcation line, they turned their attention to agenda item three, providing for arrangements to supervise the cease-fire. In its initial proposal, the UNC delegation outlined strong steps to guard against any military buildup on the peninsula after an

> **MILITARY ARMISTICE COMMISSION**
>
> According to the terms of the armistice agreement ending the Korean War, the MAC was the main agency for ensuring maintenance of the cease-fire along the new arbitrary boundary dividing the Korean peninsula. For U.S. military leaders, the creation of this body was fundamental to its plan for preserving postwar peace in Korea. At the first session of the Kaesong truce talks on July 10, 1951, Vice Admiral C. Turner Joy, the chief negotiator for the UNC, included in his proposal, as agenda item six, the determination of the composition, authority, and function of a military armistice commission. Later he provided details, recommending a body with equal representation from both sides and the power to carry out its task of ensuring respect for the armistice terms. There also would be military observation teams to serve as the eyes and ears for the MAC with the right of free and unlimited access to all of Korea. When negotiators reached a compromise on the agenda, they approved the establishment of a MAC, adding this as a provision under agenda item three, "cease-fire arrangements and inspection provisions."
>
> On December 4, 1951, negotiations focused on the details of the MAC. Although the UNC continued to insist on access throughout Korea and a predominant role for the MAC in monitoring the armistice, the Communists wanted the MAC's functions limited to the DMZ and proposed the creation of a supervisory body composed of neutral nations to monitor the cease-fire elsewhere. In sharp contrast to agenda item four on prisoner repatriation, the negotiators engaged in genuine bargaining about the MAC. This resulted in agreement that the MAC would have ten senior officers, five from each side, with overall responsibility for implementation of the terms of the armistice.

armistice, including formation of a Military Armistice Commission (MAC). After two months of discussions, disagreement on this issue and indications of disagreement on POW repatriation resulted in the negotiators moving on to agenda item five. On February 16, 1952, Joy accepted Nam Il's proposal to convene a political conference after the armistice to discuss withdrawal of foreign forces from Korea, recommendations for peaceful settlement of the Korean question, and other problems

> Its main task was to ensure that neither side exploited the cease-fire to improve its military position preparatory to resuming the fighting. Under its supervision would be ten joint military observation teams with four to six representatives. The MAC could meet daily if it wished but would convene at least once a week to consider reports of violations inside the DMZ, while forwarding all others to the Neutral Nations Supervisory Commission.
>
> On July 28, 1953, the MAC met formally for the first time on the day after the belligerents signed the armistice agreement. Initially, the body worked as anticipated and with good results. It helped determine the exact boundaries of the DMZ and supervise withdrawal of troops from that area. The MAC also set procedures for identification and checking credentials of individuals entering the DMZ. Finally, it helped in the removal of hazardous items such as mines and unexploded bombs. The MAC was unable to deal with violations, however, and cooperation on this issue soon disappeared. Whenever an incident occurred, the delegates would always hand down a split decision, guaranteeing inaction. In addition, the joint observation teams did not operate jointly. Ultimately, the UNC representatives reported that the MAC was incapable of enforcing the truce provisions or preserving the cease-fire.
>
> By 1968, there had been 250 meetings, each following a familiar pattern. The representatives would hear complaints of patrols violating the truce terms without taking action, then devote their energies to delivering charges and countercharges with denials and insults. The MAC continued to have value, however, as a conduit for communications between the commanders in times of crisis to prevent miscalculation. For example, it performed this function well in 1976 when North Koreans killed U.S. soldiers during the famous axe murder incident at Panmunjom.

relating to peace in Korea. With an end in sight, both sides engaged in bargaining that settled the specifics of inspection procedures. On April 28, the UNC delegation submitted a package proposal to resolve the remaining disputes. Abandoning the demand for prohibition of airfield rehabilitation, the UNC called for the Communist side to concede on Soviet membership on a supervisory commission and voluntary repatriation. On May 2, Nam Il formally accepted the first two provisions of the trade-off but insisted on return of all POWs, as the Geneva Convention required.[124]

For the next 15 months, the PRC and the United States refused to compromise on the issue of POW repatriation for reasons that had nothing to do with the desires of the Korean people. Fighting continued from fortified positions along a new arbitrary border that outsiders again had created, with little expectation of its removal. Despite UNC air raids on Pyongyang and hydroelectric plants at the Yalu River, the Communists would not accept voluntary repatriation, leading to an indefinite suspension of the talks in October 1952. When negotiations resumed in April 1953, Stalin was dead, and Dwight D. Eisenhower had replaced Truman as the new U.S. president. Eisenhower accelerated the UNC bombing campaign, attacking the dams and irrigation system in North Korea. Bellicose rhetoric also hinted at plans to expand the war with conventional and nuclear attacks on China. Beijing decided to break the logjam at Panmunjom because of its political vulnerability after Stalin's death and mounting economic distress. Even before the talks resumed, the Communists had accepted a UNC proposal for an exchange of sick and wounded prisoners and suggested turning nonrepatriates over to a neutral state. In late May and early June 1953, Chinese forces staged powerful attacks against positions that South Korean units were defending along the front line.[125] Far from being intimidated, Beijing thus showed that it considered final placement of Korea's new arbitrary border as a sign of its arrival as a world power.

A truce agreement ending the Korean War came on July 27,

1953, because both the PRC and the United States wanted an armistice. Washington and Beijing had grown tired of the military and economic expense, the political and military constraints, the worries about an expanded war, and the pressure from allies and the world community to end the stalemated war. Koreans on both sides of the DMZ still rejected as illegitimate the artificial border dividing their country, however. Food shortages in North Korea, coupled with an understanding that forcible reunification was no longer possible, compelled Kim Il Sung to accept this outcome. Further alienating the North Koreans, Stalin did not object when Mao refused to support Pyongyang's demand for a provision to return refugees, because this would delay achievement of an early armistice. Similarly, the United States decided that ensuring the survival of South Korea was enough to contain Soviet expansion in Asia because it contributed to the strengthening of non-Communist governments there. Rhee's release of North Korean POWs in June 1953 to scuttle the armistice sent a clear message that he remained obsessed with achieving reunification. A state of war continued on the Korean peninsula after 1953 because an arbitrary boundary alone could not achieve peace.

8

South of the Border

One week before the outbreak of the Korean War, John Foster Dulles, a foreign policy advisor to the Truman administration, traveled to the ROK on a fact-finding mission. On June 17, 1950, in a speech before the South Korean Assembly, he congratulated the ROK for proving that resisting Communist domination was not an impossible task. "As you establish here in South Korea a wholesome society of steadily expanding well-being," he predicted, "you will set up peaceful influences which will disintegrate the hold of Soviet Communism on your fellows in the north and irresistibly draw them into unity with you." Dulles's remarks reflected the Truman administration's expectation that containment in Korea would act as a liberating force. Once Asians could see the benefits of adopting the U.S. model of economic, political, and social development in places like the ROK, they would reject communism. In Korea, a U.S. diplomat wrote in 1947 that a future government in the south "would institute a whole series of necessary reforms which will so appeal to the North Koreans that their army will revolt, kill all the nasty Communists, and create a lovely liberal democracy to the everlasting credit of the U.S.A.!" U.S. leaders concluded that the Soviet Union had ordered North Korea's attack on South Korea to prevent this outcome.[126] After the Korean War, the United States again expected the ROK's success eventually to eliminate the arbitrary boundary in Korea.

Syngman Rhee was not willing to wait patiently for the peaceful reunification of Korea. In fact, he strenuously opposed a cease-fire in the Korean War after UN forces had pushed Communist troops above the thirty-eighth parallel in February 1951. He insisted that the United States launch an offensive to evict the Chinese from the north and destroy the remnants of Kim Il Sung's regime. This explains his insistence (beginning late in 1951) on returning the ROK capitol to Seoul from Pusan, doing so in August 1952 despite U.S. objections. More dramatic was Rhee's release of North Korean POWs in June 1953, a move that sought to scuttle an impending truce agreement. The United States immediately rebuked Rhee for his action but also

The People's Republic of China and the United States agreed on a truce in July, 1953, after finally tiring of the tension and expense of war. Here, Chinese and American generals meet at the Panmunjom Conference to discuss the terms of the armistice.

essentially met his terms for accepting an armistice. These conditions included a 90-day time limit on the postwar political conference, military assistance to equip 20 ROK divisions, massive economic aid, and a mutual defense treaty. Nevertheless, Rhee's government refused to sign the armistice agreement, hinting that it would undertake independent military action to remove Korea's arbitrary boundary regardless of cost. The Eisenhower administration was determined to prevent Rhee from reigniting the war. In August 1953, Dulles, now secretary of state, traveled to Seoul and finalized the terms for a permanent alliance. He also reiterated U.S. intentions to meet Rhee's other demands. Washington's resorting to bribery ultimately gained Rhee's support, and, in January 1954, the U.S. Senate ratified the U.S.-ROK Mutual Defense Treaty.[127]

South Korea had already shifted its strategy to demanding a

diplomatic agreement, leading to the prompt establishment of ROK control over all of Korea. During negotiations at Panmunjom from October to December 1953, the Rhee government was inflexible on this issue, hoping to create a deadlock that would force a return to war. North Korea was just as intransigent, demanding Soviet participation and a central role for Asian neutrals in a postwar conference to decide Korea's future. Talks ended when the ROK delegate stormed out of the final meeting. Any agreement removing the artificial border that divided the peninsula meant that one Korean government would disappear. Negotiators again sought an answer to this central dilemma when the Geneva Conference convened in April 1954 in accordance with the terms of the armistice agreement. Rhee threatened to boycott, but the United States bought Rhee's participation with a pledge of more military aid. Discussion shifted to the crisis in Indochina after there was failure to agree on the steps necessary to achieve a permanent political settlement in Korea. Rhee then visited the United States, criticizing the Eisenhower administration for entertaining compromises at Geneva, urging renewed war in Korea, and calling for a crusade to destroy the Communists. In August 1955, he announced that the ROK would ignore the armistice. Thereafter, Rhee regularly issued public threats about staging an offensive northward to reunify the peninsula.[128]

South Korea faced a daunting challenge in meeting grandiose U.S. expectations, because in July 1953 it was a nation in ruins. Three years of war had destroyed 600,000 homes, 4,000 schools, and 17,000 plants and business facilities. Estimates of property damage exceeded $2 billion. The ROK's gross national product had declined 14 percent from 1949 to 1952, with agricultural output, the mainstay of the prewar southern economy, dropping 27 percent. President Rhee understood that economic growth was the key to the ROK's survival as well as to his hopes of achieving reunification. Recognizing his lack of managerial skills, he immediately appointed "technocrat ministers" who possessed economic expertise and management ability. Inflation was the greatest initial impediment to economic recovery, as prices increased 500 percent in 1951 alone. The government proposed spending cuts and tax increases, but the assembly was not entirely cooperative.

Rhee also devoted attention to the revitalization of the coal industry. Government mines produced 77 percent of South Korea's coal in 1953, but output had been in a state of steady decline. A task force of civilian and army experts reversed this

THE GENEVA CONFERENCE

The Geneva Conference, an international conference to discuss questions regarding the future of Korea and French Indochina, began in Geneva, Switzerland on April 26, 1954. Not only did it fail to remove the artificial border dividing the Korean peninsula, but also it ironically resulted in imposition of a new arbitrary boundary across Vietnam. All UN members that had sent troops to fight in the Korean War—except South Africa—attended the discussions on Korea, as did the Republic of Korea, the Democratic People's Republic of Korea, the People's Republic of China, and the Soviet Union. It was the last major occasion during which the postwar international community exerted influence to achieve reunification of Korea. The conference was the first chance for China's new Communist government to establish itself as a major actor in international politics. The United States responded with hostility, refusing to recognize Beijing's legitimacy and denigrating its status. These U.S. attempts, however, proved futile because all others at the conference understood that it was critical for the PRC to be a central player to resolve the issues.

The Geneva Conference was held in accordance with the armistice agreement that ended the Korean War in July 1953. That agreement had provided that three months after the truce became effective, a political conference would convene to achieve the withdrawal of all foreign troops and the peaceful settlement of the Korean question. A meeting was held in Korea at Panmunjom in October 1953 to accomplish this objective, but negotiations broke down in December. World leaders then decided at a foreign ministers' meeting in Berlin during February 1954 that a conference would meet in Geneva to seek a peaceful settlement of the Korean issue. When discussions trend in 1954, resulting in a 44 percent increase in production in 1955 and a double-digit rate annually until 1960. To be sure, an arbitrary boundary prevented access to hydroelectric power in the north, limiting southern gains in power output to spur industrialization; however, the ROK delayed the formulation of a plan for economic development in anticipation of reunification.[129]

South Korea benefited during the postwar period from major U.S. economic aid, amounting to $200 million annually. It turned to Korea on May 22, the ROK representatives submitted a 14-point proposal that included three major provisions. First, all sides would accept the authority of the UN to resolve the Korean problem. Second, there would be free elections under supervision of the UN for the purpose of creating a united, independent, and democratic Korea. Third, UN forces would remain in Korea until the UN had accomplished this mission. The Communist delegations rejected this formula. The Soviet counterproposal had five points, with withdrawal of all foreign troops from the Korean peninsula taking precedence over all other provisions. Because neither side would compromise, negotiations on Korea's future became deadlocked.

On June 15, the 16 nations that had fought on the UN side in the Korean War issued a declaration stating that the UN had full authority to take collective action to repel aggression, to restore peace and security, and to provide its good offices to achieve a peaceful settlement in Korea. Also, the declaration stated that there should be truly free elections under UN supervision for the purpose of establishing an all-Korean national assembly in which representation would be in direct proportion to the indigenous population in the north and the south. That day, discussions on Korea closed with the country still divided and with opposing forces still facing each other across the arbitrary boundary at the DMZ. Thereafter, the UN General Assembly annually reaffirmed this "Geneva formula" for the reunification of Korea. Meanwhile, there was progress toward a settlement on Indochina, largely because France wanted to withdraw after its defeat at the hands of the Vietminh at Dien Bien Phu in April. The Soviets and Chinese persuaded Ho Chi Minh to accept the Geneva Accords of 1954, resulting in an artificial border dividing Vietnam.

peaked in 1956 at $356 million. Until 1960, U.S. funds composed half of the ROK's budget. Added assistance for economic recovery and development in postwar South Korea came from the United Nations Korean Reconstruction Agency (UNKRA). The UN had created the UNKRA in December 1950 to supervise nationwide economic recovery in a united Korea when there was still hope for removal of the arbitrary border dividing the peninsula despite evidence of Chinese intervention. The UNKRA began work as mandated six months after the armistice, but in South Korea alone. Initially, it provided basic relief in the form of food, clothing, and other types of aid totaling $26 million. The UNKRA then implemented a full-scale recovery program that included fertilizer and irrigation projects, classroom construction, and rehabilitation of the fishing industry. It also provided expertise and capital for industrial growth. When the UNKRA finished its work in June 1958, it had spent $140 million and sponsored 4,800 economic projects.[130] Yet South Korea's economy remained depressed and underdeveloped. Rhee was responsible for this economic stagnation. The elderly leader, at nearly 80 years old, concentrated his attention during the 1950s on consolidating his political power. He relied on the police and army for control, using both against his opponents.[131]

South Korea made little progress toward modernization during the 1950s because Rhee used the ROK's bureaucracy as an instrument to serve his political ambition. Loyalty was a priority, resulting in rampant corruption and tolerance of incompetence. Splitting with the Korea Democratic Party, Rhee formed a new Liberal Party that used patronage to destroy local autonomy. Constant intrigue and shifting coalitions promoted political instability, which prevented a united movement to force change in the government. Over time, Rhee developed new tactics to retain power, resorting to bribes and favors to silence his critics. He also ordered the arrest and imprisonment of critics serving in the assembly and manipulated electoral politics to retain power. This perpetuated an existing pattern that had

South Korea survived the war, but just barely, suffering billions of dollars in damage to its infrastructure and economy. However, President Syngman Rhee worked to restore the country, and he stands here proudly displaying the Korean flag outside his South Korean headquarters.

created a crisis during the Korean War. In May 1952, Rhee declared martial law and forced the assembly to approve a constitutional amendment allowing popular election of the president. Rhee easily won reelection, but martial law stayed in effect as a means to silence opposition. He resorted to this same subtle form of violence in 1955 because the constitution limited the president to two terms. When balloting in the assembly for an amendment to delete the provision fell short of the two-thirds needed for passage by one-third of a vote, the speaker declared the fraction "rounded off," and the measure passed. Rhee again won easy reelection in 1956, but Chang Myon, his most vocal critic, was elected his vice president, indicating increasing public opposition.[132]

Rhee relied on North Korea's threat to South Korea to justify his dictatorial rule. During the Korean War, the ROK army had implemented a major military campaign, code-named Operation Ratkiller, to wipe out guerrilla warfare in the ROK. Insurgents operating in South Korea in June 1950 had received reinforcements after the Inchon landing trapped North Korean troops in the south, resulting in intensified raids against UN positions after battle lines stabilized in November 1951. Conducted in four stages from December 1951 to March 1952, Operation Ratkiller killed or captured more than 30,000 Communist guerrillas in the southern and central ROK. Excessive force and brutality characterized this campaign, as police and right-wing youth groups participated.[133] Naturally, the ROK government implemented strong measures after the Korean War to punish anyone even suspected of Communist sympathies in South Korea. Opposition to Communist ideology and hostility toward North Korea were basic features of the ROK's educational system. Increasingly, however, Rhee exploited anticommunism as a device to strengthen authoritarianism. In December 1958, the assembly debated a new National Security Law that outlawed derogatory statements against Rhee, threatening violators with imprisonment. Opponents staged a sit-down strike to block passage, but police removed them from the building, and the remaining legislators approved the bill.[134]

By 1960, Rhee's dilapidated democracy teetered on the brink of collapse. Unable to enlist capable advisors, the aged leader had to make major decisions alone, resulting in a pattern of confusion and indecision. The opposition Democratic Party held one-third of the seats in the assembly, which was enough to block passage of constitutional amendments. There was infighting in the Liberal Party regarding Rhee's successor as well as revelations of scandal surrounding the diversion of U.S. aid to private use.

Disunity eliminated any hope that Rhee would survive political protests in April 1960 when he relied on police interference and gross fraud to engineer Vice President Chang Myon's lopsided defeat for reelection. Thousands of students joined demonstrations that climaxed in a march on the presidential mansion, where police fired on protesters and killed 200 people. Rhee declared martial law, but the army refused to defend him. Intense U.S. pressure persuaded Rhee to resign and flee to Hawaii. South Koreans then ratified a new constitution providing for a parliamentary system that empowered the assembly to elect a prime minister who would exercise executive authority. The Democratic Party swept the May elections, winning the majority of seats necessary to elect its leader, Chang Myon, as prime minister.[135]

Significantly, Korea's arbitrary boundary was a major reason for the death of the ROK's first democratically elected government. Factional rivalries immediately emerged after the removal of limits on civil liberties. Average South Korean citizens not familiar with open political competition were alarmed when small left-wing parties formed. With memories of the Korean War still fresh, political debate about whether to support North Korean reunification proposals raised questions about the risks of continuing democratic rule. Worse, the government tolerated increasing domestic instability, failing to restrict radical student activism or punish irresponsible newspaper reporting. Democracy seemed to mean aimlessness, weakness, and inefficiency. With the police demoralized, the army filled the political vacuum that fueled popular insecurity. Most important, South Koreans were afraid that the DPRK would exploit the ROK's weakness to impose Communist rule. On May 16, 1961, General Pak Chong-hui led a group of junior army officers in seizing power. After dissolving the assembly, Pak forced Chang Myon to resign and established a supreme council to supervise national reconstruction. South Koreans and the United States welcomed the restoration of order, and the ROK assembly lacked the power and the resolve to prevent the coup.[136]

For the next two decades, Pak Chong-hui consolidated his position as military dictator of the ROK. A new Korean Central Intelligence Agency (KCIA) would become a key weapon in squashing dissent. Pak first ruled by decree, issuing a new law to allow for political repression in the name of anticommunism. His edicts swept petty criminals and hoodlums from city streets, imprisoned corrupt politicians, and punished scheming businessmen. Pak forced approval of constitutions in 1963 and 1972 that gave him total authority. South Koreans accepted random arrests, illegal imprisonment, and press censorship because they believed that defense against the DPRK required a strong leader and a powerful military. Moreover, Pak implemented a series of economic development plans that exceeded all expectations. Rapid industrialization fueled an increase in exports, and a "New Village Movement" revitalized rural areas and modernized the agricultural sector. The ROK's gross national product increased ten percent annually, and per capita income rose 300 percent during the decade after 1965. Authoritarianism made possible mobilization of the populace to achieve unprecedented prosperity and to transform the ROK into an economic giant. As their standard of living improved, however, South Koreans began to want political freedom. High unemployment rates and low industrial wages created new social strains, as the width of the arbitrary border dividing rich and poor steadily expanded.[137]

Pak Chong-hui was never able to eliminate opposition to his dictatorship, despite resorting to the use of spies to monitor political dissidents, torture to extract confessions, fixed trials to justify repression, and a brutal crackdown on student activists. His most effective critic was Kim Dae-jung, a charismatic populist leader who had almost defeated Pak in the 1971 presidential election. Two years later, KCIA agents abducted Kim in Tokyo, secretly returned him to Seoul, and placed him under house arrest preparatory to a trial on charges of treason. Loud protests at home and from abroad compelled Pak to release him and apologize to Japan. South Koreans were having greater difficulty accepting the need for dictatorial rule given the ROK's booming economy and U.S. President Richard M. Nixon's policy of détente with both the Soviet Union and the PRC. Popular demands for democracy had grown in response to former president Jimmy Carter's criticism of Pak's dictatorship. Previously, the United States had tolerated Pak because South Korea under his leadership was no longer a financial burden dependent for its survival on U.S. economic and military assistance, which by 1976 had totaled $12.5 billion. Young South Koreans blamed the United States for preventing democracy in the ROK, however. By 1978, Pak faced stronger opposition in the assembly, a mounting number of union strikes, and angry student demonstrations. In October 1979, his KCIA chief assassinated the ROK president during dinner.[138]

Military dictatorship in the ROK had strengthened the arbitrary boundary dividing Korea. In fact, South Korea had not developed a credible reunification strategy since the end of the Korean War. During the 1950s, the Rhee government consistently emphasized the building of its armed forces, transforming the ROK's military establishment into one of the most powerful in Asia. Rhee's calls to "March North" were rhetorical bluster, however, because the deterrent alliance with the United States precluded aggressive action. Chang Myon advanced a proposal in 1960 for UN-supervised nationwide elections based on the principle of "one person, one vote." The weakness of his government caused most South Koreans to view this as a formula that would allow the DPRK to absorb the ROK. After seizing power in 1961, Pak Chong-hui adopted a strategy calling for "construction first, unification later."[139]

Despite economic development, North Koreans had little incentive to emulate the South Korean model so long as a capitalist ROK crushed dissent. Events in the aftermath of Pak's assassination showed how military dictatorship had strengthened Korea's arbitrary boundary. General Chun Du-hwan seized power in South Korea and declared martial law, moving quickly to blunt moves toward democratic reform and gain dictatorial power for himself. Then, in May 1980, he sent South Korean special forces to the southwestern city of Kwangju to suppress antigovernment protests against the imposition of martial law. In the violence that followed, ROK troops killed about 200 people.[140]

Economic development, however, altered dramatically the dynamics of the debate over how to eliminate Korea's artificial border. In February 1982, the Chun government advanced a new proposal calling for formation of a consultative conference to adopt "confidence-building" measures, setting the stage for reunification. Increasing pressure on the DPRK to accept, Chun began to initiate liberalization policies, such as allowing dismissed student dissidents and professors to return to campus, ending limits on political activities, and releasing political prisoners. His actions in part reflected a need to create a favorable political environment in preparation for the 1988 Olympic Games in Seoul. He also wanted to win the general election in 1985 and thereby give his regime legitimacy. Dissidents only escalated opposition, however, demanding a constitutional amendment to allow for popular election of the president. In 1986, they initiated a national petition campaign, but Chun announced his determination to preserve the existing constitution and endorsed former general No Tae-u to replace him as president. In June 1987, mass demonstrations erupted nationwide, with more than four million citizens participating. Police efforts to suppress them were overwhelmed by the demonstrators in many cities.[141]

An overwhelming majority of South Koreans seemed prepared to participate in a violent revolution to sweep aside the artificial barriers to democracy in the ROK. Also, the United States was pressing Chun to enact democratic reforms. On June 29, No issued "South Korea's Democracy Declaration," which promised direct presidential elections, amnesty for Kim Dae-jung, local governmental autonomy, and freedom of the press. A popular referendum approved the new constitution in October, setting the stage for No's election as president after three other candidates split the opposition vote. Opposition parties, however, soon achieved majority status in the national assembly. After assuming office in February 1988, No Tae-u acted to exploit the ROK's economic power and new democratic credentials, implementing a foreign policy labeled "Nordpolitik" that called for reconciliation with Pyongyang, Moscow, and Beijing. This resulted in normalization of relations with the Soviet Union in 1990 and the PRC in 1992. No's strategy led to an agreement with the DPRK to begin to consider the adoption of confidence-building measures.[142]

During 1990, the two Koreas discussed steps toward eliminating the arbitrary boundary dividing the peninsula in a series of high-level meetings that sought to repeat events in Germany that same year. For South Koreans, the absence of dramatic progress toward reunification thereafter was not just a disappointment but something of a surprise. In their search for an explanation for the failure to achieve prompt amalgamation, many pointed an accusing finger at the United States. A 1988 poll found that nearly half of all university students in the ROK considered the United States "the greatest impediment to Korea's reunification."[143] Because all Koreans desperately desired national unity, foreign involvement offered a simple and powerful explanation, as it had in the past, for Korea's ongoing tragedy. This belief allowed South Koreans to ignore the fact that the inability to accomplish quick reunification derived from the fundamental and profound differences separating the two Koreas. North Korea had a socialist economy, a regimented society, and an unusual totalitarian political structure. In sharp contrast, South Korea had a capitalist economy, an increasingly open society, and a democratic political system. Unlike Germany, Korea's arbitrary border was symbolic of the division between two thoroughly different models of development that was in no way artificial.

9

North of the Border

After 1953, the DPRK recognized neither the permanence of the armistice line nor the legitimacy of the ROK. Pyongyang claimed to be the only government of all Korea and had considerable historical evidence to underscore its case. The DPRK can date its origins to August 1945, with the creation of the Committee for the Preparation of Korean Independence under leftist leader Yo Un-hyong, on the day Japan surrendered in World War II. After forming the body on the advice of the Japanese governor, Yo immediately set about creating 135 local "people's committees" to assume administrative responsibilities in liberated Korea. Most Koreans accepted Yo's authority, including landlords, intellectuals, students, and professional people. By the end of August, Yo had emerged as the unchallenged de facto leader of all of Korea. Soviet forces occupying the area north of the thirty-eighth parallel earlier that month had recognized his authority, leading to Yo's establishment of the KPR as his nation's new government. When U.S. forces landed at Inchon early in September, however, the U.S. occupation commander instantly rejected the legitimacy of the KPR. Thereafter, the people's committees would survive only in North Korea, where they would provide the structural foundation for what Kim Il Sung would proclaim three years later as the national government of Korea.[144]

Circumstances on both sides of Korea's arbitrary border after the Korean War at first supported the DPRK's claim to be the only legitimate national government. North Korea had a stronger political, economic, and social system than the ROK for at least two decades after the armistice. The DPRK's ability to establish its superiority was even more remarkable because military occupation and merciless U.S. bombing had reduced the area north of the DMZ to almost a barren wasteland. Immediate challenges in postwar North Korea included a serious manpower shortage. By 1953, the population had declined by 1.3 million as a consequence of wartime casualties and refugees fleeing south. There was a huge deficiency of able-bodied males at a time when the demand for manpower for economic reconstruction was most acute. Policies for reconstruction focused first on the achievement of mechanization to overcome the labor shortage, reinforcing a prewar emphasis on industrialization. The government offered incentives for developing labor-saving devices and created training programs to increase the number of technical personnel. The government also provided child care to maximize use of women in the workplace, as well as upgrading health and sanitation to keep laborers on the job.[145]

North Korea received significant assistance from the Soviet Union for economic recovery after the Korean War. Moscow provided the DPRK with money, advisors, and equipment to enact a series of five-year plans that nationalized industry and collectivized farms. Achievement of Stalinist social regimentation promoted great economic strides prior to 1960, including dramatic expansion and diversification of industry. North Korea produced increasing amounts of machine tools, autos, tractors, mining equipment, and chemicals. Despite the failure to achieve agricultural self-sufficiency, living standards in the north were superior to those in South Korea. More rapid urbanization and better education contributed to the emergence of a large and well-trained industrial and clerical workforce. Pyongyang devoted a preponderance of its resources to maintaining a large military establishment, which included an army of 350,000 soldiers equipped with modern weapons. Naturally, the Rhee regime's constant references to the need to "March North" provided the DPRK with a way to justify its actions. If an opportunity emerged, however, Pyongyang wanted the capacity to remove the artificial border dividing Korea by resorting to force. During the 1950s, Soviet and Chinese opposition to resumption of the Korean War meant that forcible reunification was nothing more than a theoretical option.[146]

Communist rule guaranteed unquestioned obedience of the people of North Korea in the implementation of government plans for postwar reconstruction. Less certain was who would become the DPRK's permanent leader. Kim Il Sung had been premier since 1948 and chair of the Korean Workers' Party

(KWP) in 1949. Initially, he had shared power with other factions, including the indigenous Communists, Soviet Koreans, and those who had completed the "Long March" with Chinese leader Mao Zedong. Kim Il Sung faced the challenge of political consolidation after the Korean War because his failed attempt at forcible reunification had devastated the north physically and killed millions of Koreans. Moreover, he lost effective control of wartime decision-making after Chinese intervention late in 1950, although he retained authority over the government and the army. Kim Il Sung skillfully exploited popular hatred and fear of American aggression to consolidate his power. His postwar priority of industrial relocation reflected this strategy. Japan had built most plants on the west and east coasts because raw materials were transported from distant colonial possessions. Because these were easy targets for U.S. attack during the war, the DPRK built new industrial facilities inland and underground based on Kim's constant reminders about the certainty of a new American invasion.[147]

Kim Il Sung prevailed in a series of postwar power struggles because he was able to make his rivals the scapegoats for wartime failures. He pointed especially to the false predictions that there would be a popular uprising against the Rhee regime in response to an invasion. Pak Hon-yong, the DPRK foreign minister, had also said that 200,000 Communist guerrillas in the south would join the fight. If insurrections had occurred, Kim Il Sung argued, "we could have liberated Pusan and prevented the Americans from landing"[148] at Inchon. Kim focused on Pak, who had led the clandestine operations of the Communist underground against the Japanese during the colonial era. Not only were his revolutionary credentials superior to Kim's, but also he was the DPRK's leading ideologue.

In July 1953, Kim Il Sung had Pak and 12 of his allies arrested for treason. Charges at trial held that they were spies for the "American imperialists" and had committed wanton murders of "patriotic" cadres to preserve a conspiracy to topple the Communist government. Swiftly convicted, ten received the death sentence and quick execution. Two others would serve long prison terms. Pak Hong-yong was tried, convicted, and executed in 1956. Had there not been a sworn enemy south of Korea's arbitrary border, Kim Il Sung would never have been able to establish himself as North Korea's "Supreme Leader."[149]

Having disposed of Pak's domestic faction, Kim Il Sung began to transform North Korea into a classic Stalinist state and complete his consolidation of power. In 1956, the Chinese and Soviet factions challenged Kim Il Sung's bid for unchallenged power after Moscow's adoption of destalinization. Kim then exploited this new act of alleged treason to purge the KWP, blaming this disloyalty on hasty wartime recruitment of 400,000 new members. "An overwhelming majority of [the new members] were young in terms of both the level of political consciousness and practical experience,"[150] he explained. Most "could barely read the Korean alphabet." They had supported the UNC during occupation, and many joined the refugee exodus southward late in 1950. Kim Il Sung initiated a new coercive program that increased membership 300 percent to 12 percent of the 10.7 million people in North Korea in 1961. This facilitated party imposition of Stalinist programs and allowed for exploitation of political agitation to bolster Kim's authority. Kim Il Sung also regimented education and linked a revival of Korean nationalism to support for socialism. Central to the success of his strategy was a pattern of increasing isolation. The Communist government imposed restrictions that denied the North Korean people access to any outside information. Korea's arbitrary border made it possible for Kim Il Sung to transform the DPRK into an almost completely closed society.[151]

In 1972, the DPRK adopted a new constitution that provided the foundation for the emergence of a cult of personality in North Korea that would have make Soviet leader Joseph Stalin blush. Kim Il Sung retained his prior party posts as general secretary of the Central Committee and chair of the Military Commission. He resigned as premier to assume the newly created office of president.[152] Kim Il Sung now was in a position where he could satisfy an obsession with achieving national self-reliance under his absolute supreme rule. In 1955, he had enunciated the *juche* ideology to provide guidance in achieving this goal. A fundamental tactic that Kim Il Sung used to mobilize the people to reach self-reliance was systematic exploitation of memories of the war. Of utmost importance was maintaining mass hatred and fear of the United States. In May 1972, Kim Il Sung stated the case succinctly, when he declare that his people

> have strong anti-U.S. sentiments because they suffered great damage at the hands of the U.S. imperialists during the war.... Since the situation is tense, we cannot but continue stepping up preparations for war. We make no secret of this. Who can guarantee that the U.S. imperialists will not attack this country again? *What is most important in our preparations is to educate all the people to hate U.S. imperialism* [as cited]. Otherwise, we will not be able to defeat the U.S. imperialists who boast of their technological superiority.

An example of how the DPRK used memories of the war to build popular support for the regime was the displaying of evidence of U.S. wartime atrocities at a museum at Sinchon.[153]

Pyongyang created massive fabrications of history to bolster the government's authority. Most important, the DPRK insisted for a half-century that the ROK had started the Korean War, always reiterating Kim Il Sung's public explanation of June 26, 1950: "The army of the puppet government of the traitor Syngman Rhee started an all-out offensive against the areas of the northern half of the Republic all along the 38th parallel." Kim Il Sung added to his historical revisionism in August 1953:

> The heroic struggle waged by the Korean people for three years in defense of the country's freedom and independence against the U.S. imperialist armed invaders ended in victory for us. The U.S. imperialist aggressors suffered an ignominious defeat in their military adventure to turn our country into their colony and enslave the Korean people. The enemy was compelled to sign the Armistice Agreement.[154]

Another objective of the Communist regime's manipulation of the historical record was to lay the groundwork for elevating Kim Il Sung's position to that of *suryong*, or "great leader." The DPRK used thought control techniques far more pervasive than what Mao Zedong pioneered in the PRC to persuade the North Korean people of Kim's infallibility. Furthermore, juche required absolute loyalty to one leader as an essential for realization of self-reliance. By the 1980s, educational indoctrination and ceaseless propaganda had conditioned the North Korean people to attribute literally every success, in their words, to the brilliance of the "Great Leader" Kim Il Sung.[155]

JUCHE

After the Korean War, *juche* became the ruling ideology in the DPRK and a powerful force strengthening the existence of the arbitrary boundary dividing the peninsula. Also known as "Kim Il Sung-ism" after its originator, it came to dominate every aspect of life in North Korea, from foreign policy to routine lifestyle. Resembling an absolute religious dogma, juche consisted of four main concepts—self-determination in ideology, independence in politics, self-reliance in economics, and self-defense in military affairs. Commonly referred to as the concept of self-reliance, the word "*juche*" first appeared when Kim Il Sung purged his political opponents, notably Pak Hon-yong, in the course of power struggles after the armistice ended the fighting in Korea in July 1953. Kim severely criticized the Chinese and Soviet factions for following the teachings of Marxism-Leninism dogmatically. Instead, he insisted on developing and adopting a Korean version of Marxism-Leninism, which allegedly harmonized with the realities of the Korean situation.

Kim Il Sung developed juche in response to Soviet patron Joseph Stalin's refusal and Chinese leader Mao Zedong's reluctance to intervene in the Korean War in October 1950 to prevent advancing U.S. forces from destroying the DPRK. The ideology provided guidance for creating a North Korea that was strong enough to avoid dependence on either Beijing or Moscow. In 1982, Kim Jong Il, Kim Il Sung's son, redefined the ideology into a political philosophy. In *On Juche Ideology*, he described it as containing six propositions: (1) "Man is the master of all things and man decides everything";

North Korea's foreign policy began to display independence and inconsistency even before Pyongyang's public commitment to achieving self-reliance. Chinese military intervention in the Korean War had resulted in Beijing's replacing Moscow as the DPRK's primary patron at the time of the armistice. Kim Il Sung was happy to accept economic, military, and diplomatic support from either Communist power, but not if the price was perpetuation of dependence. Emergence of the Sino-Soviet dispute during the late 1950s provided him with leverage to assert the DPRK's autonomy. Assuming an initial posture of neutrality, Pyongyang signed a security pact with both the Soviet Union

> (2) self-reliance is the soul of human existence; (3) "all behaviors of man in historical development are decided by his ideological consciousness, and only when the masses of the working class people are guided by ideological consciousness can they become the masters of their destinies and the mighty creators of history"; (4) the masses of the working class are the prime movers of revolution and construction; (5) revolution in one's country should be central to the thinking and revolutionary action of all men; (6) the masses of the working class people should take a masterly attitude with regard to revolution and construction because they are the masters.
>
> Both Kims used juche as a political tool to justify North Korea's political system, the government structure, and the personality cult of father and son. Juche has played a key role in the process of consolidating the North Korean political power structure and prevented the collapse of the DPRK, despite severe economic hardships beginning in the 1990s. Moreover, juche ideology was used as a tool to prepare the theoretical foundation to support the junior Kim's replacement of his father as suryong, or maximum leader. Originally, North Korean leaders established this socialist state on the orthodox socialist principle that placed the party above all else. The DPRK's ruling hierarchy developed juche to transform North Korea into a unique type of a Communist state where the leader reigns supreme over the party. North Korea's implementation of this father-to-son power succession plan has made the DPRK a target of criticism among socialists.

Following the war, North Korean leader Kim Il Sung, seen here, acquired complete, unchallenged power. Following Stalin's lead, he imposed restrictive programs that increased the government's authority and made North Korea a closed, Communist society.

and the PRC. A residue of hostility toward Moscow for not providing enough help in the Korean War to remove the arbitrary boundary dividing the nation caused the DPRK in 1962 to align closely with the PRC after the Cuban Missile Crisis.

For the next two years, Pyongyang and Moscow waged a propaganda battle in *Nodong Shinmun* and *Pravda*, their respective state newspapers. The DPRK charged that during the war, the Soviets "sold us materials at prices far above the world market, while taking away from us in return many tons of gold, huge quantities of precious metals, and other raw materials at below-market prices." Pyongyang also identified with the Chinese advocacy of revolutionary nationalism in a global campaign against U.S. imperialism.[156]

After 1965, the DPRK concentrated on projecting an image as the champion of underdeveloped nations. It displayed growing militancy and belligerence in response to U.S. military intervention in Vietnam. In January 1968, North Korean ships captured the U.S.S. *Pueblo*, a surveillance vessel operating near Wonsan. Pyongyang incarcerated the captain and crew for over a year, subjecting them to torture and indiscriminate brutality. Kim Il Sung's motive may have been to reassert his unchallenged political authority in reaction to internal grumbling about economic stagnation and diplomatic irrelevance. His ability to defend the nation against the United States would demonstrate the need to implement fully the ideological precepts of juche.[157]

The PRC applauded North Korea's defiant behavior, becoming its enthusiastic sponsor. Frequent exchanges of high-level officials followed, with Kim Il Sung visiting Beijing over a dozen times. The DPRK would shift its stance in 1972 after President Richard M. Nixon's trip to China. Moving toward reconciliation, Pyongyang issued a communiqué pledging to end propaganda against South Korea, avoid provocations, and pursue removal of Korea's arbitrary border through peaceful means. It even suggested the creation of a "hot line" with Seoul to avoid miscalculations that might lead to war. These initiatives won the DPRK permanent observer status at the UN in May 1973. A dramatic reversal came just three years later, when North Korean border guards attacked U.S. soldiers and murdered them with axes in the DMZ.[158]

North Korea's policy toward South Korea has reflected the same unpredictability. In 1948, the DPRK began a policy of refusing to have any official contact with the ROK. Chinese military withdrawal in 1958, however, provided the backdrop for

Pyongyang to propose the opening of trade relations, contingent on U.S. military withdrawal. If accepted, this would be the first step toward nationwide elections and reunification. Two years later, Kim Il Sung proposed establishment of the Confederal Republic of Koryo. On both occasions, Seoul was in political turmoil and made no response. Thereafter, Pyongyang resumed its military emphasis, with frequent instigation of provocative acts. In addition to military clashes along the DMZ, DPRK warships harassed and captured southern fishing boats. After the last major border incident in October 1981, South Korea found tunnels under the DMZ that North Korea presumably had dug in preparation for a future invasion.

Periodic efforts to destabilize the ROK were another ingredient of Pyongyang's long-term strategy to eliminate Korea's arbitrary boundary that reflected its sense of superiority. In January 1968, for example, North Korean military officers raided the presidential residence on a failed mission to assassinate Pak Chong-hui. The DPRK later resorted to terrorism. In October 1983, North Korean commandos exploded a bomb in Rangoon, killing 19 people, including four ROK cabinet members. Four years later, North Korean agents were responsible for the bombing of Korean Airlines Flight 858.[159]

Simultaneously, both the DPRK and the ROK regularly offered proposals aimed at reconciliation, but none generated movement toward implementation. Pyongyang's consistent position was that there could be no progress in negotiations until U.S. troops had withdrawn from the peninsula. Seoul rejected not only this demand but also the DPRK's insistence on direct bilateral talks with the United States. After 1980, the ROK's steadily improved world position placed pressure on an increasingly isolated North Korea to compromise. In 1983, representatives from the PRC arrived in Seoul for the first time to resolve an airplane hijacking incident, opening the way for "tennis diplomacy," with a South Korean team traveling to China the next year. In 1988, both the PRC and the Soviet Union participated in the Seoul Olympic Games. With Soviet-American relations improving after 1985, Pyongyang moderated its harsh rhetoric against the United States. North Korean representatives even joined in intermittent talks with U.S. diplomats in Beijing. The ROK reciprocated with a tempering of its militant anticommunism after Communist regimes in Eastern Europe collapsed in 1989. Pyongyang's recognition that South Koreans would not abandon a system that had created unprecedented prosperity led to its proposal of confederation as a way to remove Korea's arbitrary boundary.[160]

After 1987, Pyongyang saw leverage in the radical student movement in South Korea that had grown in strength after the ROK's embrace of democracy. Young South Koreans openly criticized the government and expressed sympathy toward North Korea. Pressure for significant movement toward uniting Korea became intense after the fall of the Berlin Wall in 1989, resulting in Pyongyang and Seoul agreeing to several high-level meetings to discuss steps toward reunification. A Korean proverb—*tong-sang i-mong*—aptly described the negotiations in September 1990 when the prime ministers met for the first time in Seoul. This saying means "same bed, different dream." Both sides accepted proposals for a public declaration of nonaggression, the installation of hot lines between military commands, an end to slander and vilification in official government pronouncements, and the removal of all military equipment from the DMZ.

The North Korean delegation made further progress contingent on resolving three issues. First, the DPRK demanded that the ROK drop its proposal for the admission of both Koreas to the UN, accepting instead its plan for sharing a single seat. Second, Pyongyang insisted on the release of a student dissident and two clergymen convicted of violating an ROK law prohibiting visits to the north. Finally, the DPRK demanded immediate termination of the annual "Team Spirit" U.S.-ROK joint military exercises.[161]

South Korea rejected the DPRK's demands but advanced a counterproposal that was consistent with its prior emphasis on the need for confidence-building measures. The ROK proposed the shelving of efforts for admission to the UN and promoted a gradual increase in the exchange of people and economic cooperation. "This," the ROK's prime minister argued, "should involve the opening of southern and northern societies to each other, leading to expanding ... cooperation to build the social, cultural, and economic foundations of a single national community."[162] In the proposal, Pyongyang and Seoul would agree to direct inter-Korean trade, joint development of resources, and reconnection of roads and rail lines between north and south. The ROK also advocated free travel by separated family members older than 60, mutual public access to radio and television, and the creation of reciprocal liaison missions in Pyongyang and Seoul. Finally, South Korea wanted both governments to agree to recognize and respect each other's political and social systems. After initiation of these measures for *political* confidence-building, *military* confidence-building would begin, culminating in arms reduction. North Korea replied that South Korea still had to satisfy its three conditions before substantive negotiations could take place. Korea's two prime ministers met twice more during 1990, but the persistence of mutual distrust that the artificial border between them had perpetuated blocked further progress.[163]

Forty years after its creation, the DPRK faced the disturbing reality that Korea's arbitrary border was perhaps the most powerful factor ensuring its survival. This would become even more evident after the Soviet Union collapsed in December 1991, as North Korea entered a period of serious socioeconomic crisis. Termination of foreign aid and several natural disasters had produced shortages of food and consumer goods. Deterioration of industrial equipment and a paralyzed educational system brought productive activities to a virtual standstill. Malnutrition and starvation destroyed families, as parents deserted children and relatives fled their villages. In April 1994, Kim Il Sung died, leaving his son and designated successor Kim Jong Il with monumental challenges. His reputation as a playboy and movie fanatic led to predictions of the DPRK's imminent collapse, but the "Dear Leader" had gained administrative experience and built a base of political support serving in various government posts. Under his leadership, the state apparatus continued to retain firm control over a populace that shifted its loyalty and adoration to Kim Jong Il. By then, even defenders of Pyongyang had acknowledged the utter failure of the DPRK's socialist system.[164] ROK officials soon realized the incredible economic and political cost of rehabilitating North Korea after reunification. Ironically, many South Koreans began to see Korea's arbitrary border as worth keeping in place, at least for a while.

10

Wish and Reality

A century after Imperial Japan robbed Korea of its independence, the Korean people still did not have the ability to define and control a single vision for the future of their country. Since 1945, an arbitrary boundary has perpetuated this national tragedy. The obsession with reunification explains the outbreak of the Korean War in June 1950, among the most destructive conflicts in human history. When the fighting ended in July 1953, more than three million Koreans had been killed, wounded, or missing. Of these, 70 percent of the casualties were civilians. The war divided an estimated ten million families, representing one-third of all households north and south. Aerial bombardment was a principal cause of destruction, both personal and material. U.S. Air Force sorties dropped a total of 386,037 tons of bombs, 32,357 tons of napalm, and 313,600 rockets. Korean and foreign soldiers on both sides committed atrocities during the early stages of the war, when invading armies occupied enemy territory. Refugees totaled five million people, with two million from South Korea. The Korean War was responsible for human suffering that defies description.[165] That millions survived was a testimony to the qualities of tenacity and resourcefulness in the Korean character. Despite their sacrifices, Koreans then had to endure the unendurable fact of a new artificial border dividing their nation.

Two Koreas developed along separate paths from 1953 until the Cold War ended in the fall of 1989. Germany's reunification the following year had a dramatic impact on Koreans, because World War II had resulted in an arbitrary boundary dividing that nation as well. Naturally, South Koreans expected that the Communist regime in the north would follow the example of East Germany and quickly collapse. The two situations were entirely different, however, especially with respect to the issue of political legitimacy. In 1945, the Soviet Union imposed a political, social, and economic system on East Germany without regard to the will of the people. Arguably, the vast majority of East Germans never thoroughly accepted Communist rule as legitimate. Once Moscow decided that it could live with a united

Germany, the reason for East Germany's existence disappeared, and its citizens were able to fulfill their long-standing desire for amalgamation with West Germany. By contrast, Communist rulers in North Korea came to power in 1945 with popular approval. Significantly, Soviet troops occupied East Germany throughout the postwar period, while the Red Army withdrew from Korea in December 1948. For more than 40 years, Kim Il Sung enjoyed genuine mass support because North Koreans believed, for better or for worse, that Communist rule was in their best interests. Because the DPRK did not rely directly on the Soviet Union for survival, expectations of its rapid demise after the Cold War were unrealistic.[166]

There were other important differences. First, and most important, Germans did not fight a war to end the arbitrary boundary that divided their nation. Second, those on the political left in East Germany had far less to fear from reunification than did those in the DPRK. West Germany tolerated left-wing political activity, and the Social Democrats held widespread popular support and considerable political power. After 1948, the ROK, following a pattern existing under prior U.S. military rule, outlawed and brutally suppressed all left-wing political activities. Third, the East German people always knew far more about life in West Germany than did North Koreans about conditions in South Korea. Magnifying this disparity was the existence of West Berlin in the heart of East Germany. Surely the presence of a "South Pyongyang" after the Korean War would have made more difficult the Communist task of maintaining dominance in the DPRK. Moreover, members of reciprocal Allied Military Liaison Missions enjoyed significant freedom of movement in the other side's portion of Germany until 1991. Finally, Germany gained reunification only after its European neighbors, especially France and the Soviet Union, decided that a united Germany no longer was a military threat. In Korea, an arbitrary boundary remained in place after 1990 despite the fact that only the PRC and Vietnam objected to reunification. Unlike in Germany, national division persisted more as a consequence of domestic rather than international factors.[167]

Despite these profound differences, German reunification provided motivation for Korean attempts in the early 1990s to transform their wish—to remove the artificial border dividing their country—into reality. Each side advocated its model for political, social, and economic organization as the preferred system for development in a united Korea. South Koreans knew that the economic strength of the ROK demonstrated its superiority. North Koreans, however, remained defiantly self-confident despite the collapse of Communist regimes throughout Europe. In reality, North Korea for some time had been suffocating under a failed socialist economic system. A poor harvest in 1991 added food shortages to insufficient fuel as the DPRK's most pressing problems. Perhaps more threatening in the long run, northerners labored in a totalitarian society that denied any opportunities for individual self-expression. Communist leaders also faced the prospect of not being able to exploit hatred and fear of the United States as a means to preclude dissent and mobilize the people behind national goals. Finally, Kim Il Sung was almost 80 years old, and death of the "Great Leader" would create a power vacuum that his son would have to fill.[168]

Late in 1990, diplomatic and economic pressures forced Pyongyang to make significant concessions. In September, the Soviet Union established diplomatic relations with the ROK. It then informed the DPRK that it would accept only hard currency for commodities such as oil. In October, the PRC signed a trade agreement with the ROK. Movement toward reconciliation between the two Koreas followed in February 1991, as Seoul and Pyongyang agreed to form joint table tennis and soccer teams to participate in international competitions. That same month, the DPRK suspended ongoing talks between their prime ministers when the United States and the ROK refused to cancel "Team Spirit" joint military exercises. In April, Soviet President Mikhail Gorbachev met for the third time in ten months with ROK President No Tae-u and announced on Cheju Island that

Moscow "would not be an obstacle" to admission of the ROK to the UN. In return, No pledged $2 billion in credit and $1 billion in direct aid. They also agreed to pursue a tenfold increase in bilateral trade, to $10 billion annually within five years.[169]

Seoul's emerging partnership with Moscow placed Pyongyang in an increasingly uncomfortable position of diplomatic isolation. Worse, Beijing informed the DPRK that the PRC would not block the ROK's entry into the UN. Forced to abandon its long-held insistence on sharing a single seat with Seoul, Pyongyang applied for admission to the international organization in May 1991. When the UN Security Council approved the applications of both Koreas in August, the ROK government was jubilant. That fall, the DPRK and the ROK agreed to resume the meetings between their prime ministers, as students from both north and south met at Korea's arbitrary boundary at the DMZ to hug and sing unification songs. Expectations for an early end to the artificial division of the peninsula were rising when North and South Korea formally joined the world body in September 1991. Seoul insisted that, like Germany, seating both Koreas in the UN would not prolong the time necessary to achieve reunification, but shorten it.[170]

At this point, evidence that the DPRK would be able to produce nuclear weapons in one to three years emerged as a new barrier to reunification. On September 14, 1991, a defector from North Korea, who had been a senior diplomat, confirmed that Pyongyang was developing nuclear weapons at two sites. Concern regarding North Korea's nuclear capabilities in fact had grown steadily since the prior April, when satellite reconnaissance had revealed construction of a heavily guarded nuclear installation at Yongbyon, 55 miles north of Pyongyang. North Korea claimed it was an electricity plant, but there were no generators outside the facility or cables emerging from it. The ROK's defense minister stated publicly that the ROK might have to stage a commando raid to destroy the nuclear plant in self-defense. The DPRK denied any interest in developing nuclear weapons and indicated its willingness to permit the

International Atomic Energy Agency (IAEA) to conduct inspections inside North Korea. Pyongyang had signed the Nuclear Non-Proliferation Treaty (NPT) in 1985 but then refused to permit IAEA inspections.[171]

Seizing the initiative, ROK President No Tae-u, in a speech at the UN in September 1991, advanced a plan to end Korea's arbitrary division that required North Korea to end its nuclear weapons program and allow inspections. In response, the DPRK broke off contacts with the IAEA, stating that the United States would have to withdraw its nuclear weapons from South Korea before it would allow inspections in North Korea. Cleverly, Washington acted to meet Pyongyang's demands. On September 27, U.S. President George H.W. Bush publicly announced that, as part of his new sweeping arms reduction initiative, the United States would remove all ground- and sea-based short-range nuclear weapons from South Korea. At the fourth meeting of the Korean prime ministers in October, the ROK insisted that the DPRK halt its nuclear weapons development program and allow inspections immediately. In reply, the DPRK set new conditions, calling for the right to inspect nuclear installations in South Korea and removal of the U.S. "nuclear umbrella" of protection for the ROK. Surprisingly, on the last day of the meeting, there was progress. Each side made concessions, with North Korea dropping its precondition of the total withdrawal of U.S. troops and South Korea agreeing to approve a nonaggression pact before an agreement formally ending the Korean War.[172]

Pyongyang's nuclear weapons program provided it with leverage in its attempts to manage economic distress and diplomatic isolation. No acted to exploit his advantage in November 1991, promising that the ROK "will not manufacture, possess, store, deploy or use nuclear weapons," if the DPRK made the same pledge. Although it had been calling for a nuclear-free Korea for years, the DPRK rejected the proposal. Meanwhile, an ROK defense ministry report expressed grave concern about the ability of the DPRK to mount crude nuclear weapons on Scud missiles. Halting its plans for gradual reduction of U.S. forces in

South Korea to 30,000 by 1995, Washington announced its intent to sell Patriot missiles to the ROK and stage a huge air show in South Korea in early 1992, including stealth fighters and antimissile weapons. Evidently, this U.S. commitment to strengthen ROK defenses had an impact. On November 27, Pyongyang issued a conciliatory official statement lauding the U.S. decision to remove nuclear weapons from South Korea. More important, the DPRK stated that it would sign an agreement regarding simultaneous inspections in both Koreas once the United States commenced complete military withdrawal. Also, Pyongyang said that it would pursue an accord with Seoul to make Korea non-nuclear.[173]

At the fifth meeting of prime ministers in December 1991, the ROK reaffirmed that there were no nuclear weapons in South Korea. If Pyongyang permitted inspections in North Korea, Seoul would allow the DPRK to inspect military and civilian installations in South Korea. Complaining of pressure for "forced inspections," the DPRK revived the preconditions of removal of the U.S. "nuclear umbrella," the signing of a treaty to denuclearize Korea, an end to Team Spirit exercises, and total U.S. withdrawal from the peninsula. A determination to remove Korea's arbitrary boundary led the prime ministers to overcome their distrust and sign the "Agreement on Reconciliation, Nonaggression, Exchange and Cooperation." Under its terms, the two Koreas renounced use of armed force or acts of terrorism against one another, as well as attempts to overthrow the other side's government. They also pledged to restore telephone and mail service, promote economic exchange, reunite separated families, rebuild rail lines and roads across the DMZ, and create a joint military commission and hot lines between military commands. Refusing to call this a peace treaty, the prime ministers noted that the Korean War would not end formally until a permanent accord had replaced the armistice agreement. Critics pointed to vague language in a key passage providing that disputes "shall be peacefully resolved through dialogue and negotiations." Worse, a North Korean official at the time stated that the

DPRK had to protect its "clean society against pollution by stinking, corrupt cultures."[174]

Ironically, Washington had become alarmed at what appeared to be the ROK's frantic quest for reunification. Motivating No's haste was a desire to boost the prospects of his ally Kim Young-sam for election as president in 1992. He also wanted to secure a place in history as his nation's reunifier, hoping to arrange a summit with Kim Il Sung for this purpose. President Bush, during a visit to Seoul in January 1992, voiced concern to No about the overly rapid pace of recent agreements. Yet Bush publicly supported No's aspirations. "The day will inevitably come when this last wound of the cold war struggle will heal," he proclaimed before the National Assembly. "Korea will be whole again."[175] Visiting the DMZ, he could not resist the chance to comment on the DPRK's precarious position, stating that North Korea was under the control of "a failed regime that produces only misery and want." Later that month, the Bush administration announced that there soon would be a meeting between U.S. and North Korean representatives in New York to discuss inspections. By early February, however, the DPRK again had stated that it would not permit access to North Korea. That summer, the IAEA determined that the DPRK had extracted plutonium from its nuclear energy facility three times since 1988.[176]

New U.S. President Bill Clinton was determined to confirm that North Korea was no longer developing nuclear weapons. He considered the imposition of sanctions against North Korea, but the ROK did not want to precipitate a crisis. Washington therefore worked for a compromise. In December 1993, the DPRK proposed routine inspections of five sites in return for adding establishment of diplomatic relations to the agenda at a third meeting. To force acceptance and divert attention from a radiochemical laboratory that the IAEA wanted to inspect, the DPRK initiated a discharge operation at one nuclear reactor on May 12, 1994, to make fuel measurements impossible. After the IAEA adopted a resolution on June 10 calling for sanctions against North Korea, the DPRK declared its withdrawal from the IAEA.

Clinton prepared to order U.S. military strikes to destroy North Korea's nuclear facilities but allowed former President Jimmy Carter to attempt mediation. His personal visit to Pyongyang resulted in North Korea's agreeing to halt its nuclear program and suspend its withdrawal from the NPT. The "Agreed Framework" provided for the DPRK to consult with the IAEA on inspections and to resume inter-Korean dialogue, whereas

> ### SUNSHINE POLICY
>
> Kim Dae-jung was elected president of the ROK in December 1997. By that time, he had established a reputation as one of Korea's greatest political dissidents and proponents of democracy. As president, Kim was committed to achieving reconciliation with the DPRK. To accomplish this objective, he formulated a "Sunshine Policy" that stressed engagement with North Korea and negotiations to develop a roadmap for Korea's future. Also, Kim established reunification as a long-term objective to reassure Pyongyang that Seoul was not trying to achieve political dominance over the entire peninsula. At first, the DPRK and its new leader Kim Jong Il were very suspicious, thinking that the ROK had a hidden agenda aimed at destabilizing Communist rule in North Korea. After 1998, however, Kim's Sunshine Policy had resulted in steadily improving relations between the two Koreas and agreement for cooperation in a number of political and economic joint ventures.
>
> In March 2000, Kim Dae-jung summarized the goals of the Sunshine Policy in a speech at the Free University of Berlin. First, the ROK wanted to assist North Korea in overcoming its economic problems through investment in infrastructure, joint business ventures, and agricultural help to end food shortages. Second, Seoul sought genuine reconciliation and cooperation with Pyongyang to end confrontation and secure peace, rather than seeking reunification. Third, Kim Dae-jung urged action to arrange the reunion of families separated as a result of the Korean War. Finally, he proposed opening a dialogue to move toward implementing the basic South-North Agreement of 1991, which called for a commitment to negotiations to resolve differences and promote peace on the peninsula. Kim Dae-jung, unlike his predecessors, set no preconditions for expanded cooperative contacts with North Korea. By 2000, Seoul was providing the DPRK with $200 million in annual economic

the United States pledged to provide fuel oil to the DPRK for electrical power and help it build light water-moderated nuclear reactors that did not produce weapons-grade waste.[177]

Complications emerged to prevent implementation of the Agreed Framework. In April 1994, Kim Il Sung died. Debate ensued about whether the United States should act to encourage a "soft" or a "hard" landing for the anticipated collapse of North

> assistance. New joint ventures included tourist visits to Kumgang Mountain and the reunion of more than 8,000 separated families. Kim Dae-jung's critics charged, however, that the Sunshine Policy was dangerous because it appeased the DPRK and prevented strong action against its development of nuclear weapons.
>
> In June 2000, the Sunshine Policy resulted in Kim Dae-jung's unprecedented meeting with Kim Jong Il in Pyongyang, leading to the ROK president's winning the Nobel Peace Prize. Presidential elections in December 2002 revealed solid public support for the approach, as No Mu-hyun won after promising to pursue even more engagement with the DPRK. Early in 2003, progress toward cooperation and reconciliation between the two Koreas continued. In February, a small tour bus convoy carrying 500 southerners inaugurated the first regularly scheduled land crossing into North Korea since division of the peninsula in 1945. One hundred elderly South Koreans would visit North Korea the next week to meet relatives they had not seen since the Korean War.
>
> Hyundai Asan, the ROK company that operated the joint tourist venture at Mount Kumgang, was about to break ground on two golf courses and a ski lift, as well as begin renovation of several North Korean hotels to more than double their lodging capacity. Hyundai already was involved in seven projects in the DPRK, including construction of railways, power plants, communications networks, and an airport. ROK and DPRK negotiators during February talks had made progress on plans to build an industrial park in the north and connect two inter-Korean railways. The Sunshine Policy therefore had succeeded in breaking down mutual suspicion and building a foundation of trust between the two Koreas.

Korea, but Kim Jong Il replaced his father without incident. Beginning late in 1995, a financial crisis in East Asia eventually replaced an economic boom with a regional collapse. South Korea's faltering economy had an impact on politics, contributing to the election late in 1997 of former dissident Kim Dae-jung as president in the midst of massive lay-offs and a request for a $57 billion loan from the International Monetary Fund. The United States, Japan, and the ROK could not reach agreement on how to fund the new energy facilities in North Korea, causing an impatient DPRK secretly to resume its nuclear program. In 1998, North Korea launched a missile into Japanese airspace, while refusing to answer U.S. questions about the purpose of an underground nuclear facility at Gumchangri. In March 1999, the DPRK finally accepted visits from U.S. inspectors to the site in return for 600,000 tons of food aid. The controversy served to reinforce the artificial boundary dividing Korea, as both the United States and South Korea struggled to determine North Korea's nuclear capabilities and ensure implementation of the Agreed Framework.[178]

Kim Dae-jung saw the achievement of reconciliation between the two Koreas as the best way to persuade the DPRK that it did not need to develop nuclear weapons. He therefore developed a "Sunshine Policy" that stressed engagement with North Korea and negotiations to formulate a roadmap for Korea's future. By 1999, Seoul and Pyongyang had expanded diplomatic contacts based on mutual trust and arranged for cooperation on assorted political and economic endeavors. The Sunshine Policy was breaking down the mutual suspicion that had kept Korea's arbitrary boundary in place for a half century. In June 2000, Kim Dae-jung's efforts led to his historic meeting in Pyongyang with Kim Jong Il, which resulted in the ROK president receiving the Nobel Peace Prize.

The Clinton administration was a strong supporter of the Sunshine Policy. Working to implement the Agreed Framework, Secretary of State Madeleine Albright visited Pyongyang in October 2000. Progress toward Korea's peaceful reunification

At the start of the 21st century, fifty years after the end of the Korean War, the arbitrary border dividing the country at the 38th Parallel remained intact. Here, a South Korean soldier stands guard near Imjingak along the border.

came to an abrupt end when George W. Bush became president in January 2001. After rejecting contacts with the DPRK, he voiced displeasure with Kim Dae-jung after he joined Russia's President Vladimir Putin in stating support for respecting the 1972 Anti-Ballistic Missile Treaty.[179] Reciprocal presidential visits over the next year did nothing to close the growing rift in U.S.-ROK relations, let alone restore South Korean confidence in the United States.

Bush delivered his January 2002 State of the Union message four months after the attacks on the World Trade Center and Pentagon on September 11, 2001. In it, he linked North Korea with terrorism, declaring that it was part of an "Axis of Evil" that included Iran and Iraq. He condemned North Korea's government for arming itself with "missiles and weapons of mass destruction, while starving its citizens."[180] His threatening remarks infuriated many South Koreans because U.S. hostility toward North Korea was a threat to peace on the peninsula. In October, the Bush administration intentionally reignited the nuclear crisis with North Korea to build international support for sanctions to achieve a regime change in Pyongyang. South Korean opposition to this U.S. policy of provocation led in December to the election of No Mu-hyun as ROK president because he advocated a relationship with North Korea based on trade and dialogue. When President No refused to join Washington in provoking Pyongyang in February 2003, Washington ignored ROK objections and announced plans to move U.S. troops from the DMZ to south of Seoul. Many South Koreans suspected that the reason was to remove the threat of artillery retaliation on U.S. forces after staging a preemptive attack on DPRK nuclear facilities.[181]

By the spring of 2004, prospects for the early reunification of Korea were bleak. In February, the United States, the DPRK, Russia, the ROK, Japan, and the PRC failed to make progress at a second round of negotiations in Beijing to resolve disagreements over North Korea's nuclear program. This dispute had halted the movement toward removal of the artificial division of Korea that had occurred during the 1990s. Developments on the peninsula after the end of the Cold War exposed the unique characteristics of Korea's arbitrary boundary. Two distinct nations in fact have emerged on the Korean peninsula, with differences in language and culture strengthening the territorial and ideological separation. This explains why Koreans cannot easily transform the wish for reunification into reality. Some Koreans talk about coexistence in a united Korea of both systems, but this can never work. One Korea inevitably will absorb the other, and no one expects the DPRK to survive. Once the North Korean people gain access to complete information about events outside Korea and become aware of the superior quality of life in the south, there can be no doubt that, given a free choice, they will seek amalgamation with South Korea. Recent reports indicate, however, that Kim Jong Il retains the overwhelming and unquestioning loyalty of North Korea's people. Until that changes, perhaps the world's most famous arbitrary border will remain and will perpetuate Korea's tragic history.

CHRONOLOGY & TIMELINE

2333 B.C.	Legendary founding of Korea by Tangun.
400 B.C.	Establishment of Ko-Choson, Korea's first identifiable state.
109 B.C.	China's Emperor Wu-Ti conquers Ko-Choson and occupies Korea.
A.D. 37	Beginning of the Three Kingdoms Era with the formation of Koguryo, later joined by Paekche and Silla.
313	Koguryo eliminates the last Chinese commandary.
369	Koguryo stages first attack on Paekche.
579	Silla king adopts Buddhism as the state religion.
668	Unification of Korea under Silla.
936	Establishment of Koryo, replacing Silla as Korea's national government.
1231	Mongol invasion begins, leading to its imposition of rule on Korea.
1392	General Yi Song-gye establishes the Choson Dynasty.
1446	King Sojong develops Hangul, Korean written language.
1592–1598	Japanese invasions of Korea.
1627–1637	Manchu invasions of Korea.
1740	Confucian examination system adopted to recruit government officials.
1783	First Korean convert to Christianity.
1839	Yi government executes three French Catholic missionaries.
1866	Koreans attack and burn the American schooner *General Sherman*; French punitive expedition loots and burns town on Kanghwa Island.
1871	U.S. punitive expedition to retaliate for Korean attacks on U.S. ships.
1876	Treaty of Kangwha signed with Japan.
1882	Treaty of Chemulpo for friendship and trade signed with the United States.
1884	Pro-Japanese modernizers stage failed coup to seize power.
1894	Tonghak Rebellion ignites Sino-Japanese War.
1895	Treaty of Shimonoseki ends China's dominant position in Korea.

CHRONOLOGY & TIMELINE

1896	Russia rejects Japan's proposal to divide Korea at the thirty-eighth parallel.
1904	Japan's attack on Russian fleet starts the Russo-Japanese War.
1905	Treaty of Portsmouth recognizes Japan's dominance over Korea; Japan imposes a protectorate on Korea.
1910	Japanese annexation of Korea.
1919	March First Movement for Korea's independence from Japan; formation of the Korean Provisional Government in Shanghai, China.
1921	Formation of the Korean Communist Party.
1943	Cairo Declaration promises independence for Korea "in due course."
1945	At the Yalta Conference, President Franklin D. Roosevelt and Soviet Premier Joseph Stalin agree to a postwar trusteeship for Korea; Soviet-American occupation of Korea and division at thirty-eighth parallel; creation of the Korean People's Republic as Korea's postwar government; Soviet-American approval of the Moscow Agreement on Korea.
1947	UN resolution provides for supervised nationwide elections in Korea.
1948	North-South Conference in Pyongyang fails to end Korea's division; establishment of the ROK; establishment of the DPRK.
1949	Violent border clashes between DPRK and ROK military units at the thirty-eighth parallel.
1950	North Korea attacks South Korea, igniting the Korean War; DPRK establishes political control over most of South Korea; Inchon landing leads to retreat of North Korean forces above the thirty-eighth parallel, defeating the DPRK's attempt to reunite Korea; ROK establishes political control over most of North Korea; Chinese People's Volunteers Army intervenes in the Korean War.
1951	Negotiations for an armistice to end the Korean War begin at Kaesong; acceptance of a DMZ as Korea's new arbitrary boundary.
1953	Armistice agreement ends the Korean War.

CHRONOLOGY & TIMELINE

1954   Geneva Conference fails to reach agreement on Korea's reunification.

1955   Kim Il Sung enunciates the ideology of juche, or self-reliance.

1956   Kim Il Sung eliminates his rivals after trials and executions for treason.

1960   Student rebellion ousts Syngman Rhee as president of the ROK; first democratically elected government assumes power in the ROK; Kim Il Sung proposes reunification as the Confederal Republic of Koryo.

1961   General Pak Chong-hui leads coup and seizes power.

1968   North Korean commandos raid presidential residence in Seoul; North Korea captures the U.S. surveillance ship Pueblo.

1971   Kim Dae-jung almost wins presidential election against Pak.

A.D. 37 — Three Kingdoms Era begins

1896 — Russia rejects Japan's proposal to divide Korea at the thirty-eighth parallel

1910 — Japanese annexation of Korea

1945 — Soviet-American occupation of Korea and division at thirty-eighth parallel

1949 — Violent border clashes at the thirty-eighth parallel

A.D. 668 — Unification of Korea under Silla

1905 — Treaty of Portsmouth recognizes Japan's dominance over Korea

1943 — Cairo Declaration promises independence for Korea "in due course"

1948 — Republic of Korea and Democratic People's Republic of Korea created

CHRONOLOGY & TIMELINE

1972	North-South declaration on Korean political unity.
1973	DPRK gains permanent observer status at UN; Korean agents seize dissident leader Kim Dae-jung in Tokyo.
1976	DPRK guards use axes to murder U.S. soldiers in the DMZ.
1979	Assassination of South Korean President Pak Chong-hui.
1980	Kwangju incident results in ROK troops killing 200 demonstrators.
1981	Discovery of tunnels that North Korea had dug under the DMZ.
1983	North Korean commandos explode a bomb in Rangoon, Thailand, that kills 19 people, including 4 ROK cabinet members.

1950
North Korea's attack on South Korea ignites the Korean War

1954
Geneva Convention fails to reach agreement for Korea's reunification

1953
Korean War armistice establishes a DMZ dividing Korea

1960
Kim Il Sung proposes reunification as the Confederal Republic of Koryo

1981
Discovery of tunnels North Korea had dug under the DMZ

1991
Agreement on Reconciliation, Nonaggression, Exchange in Pyongyang

2000
First Meeting of the presidents of the two Koreas in Pyongyang

1998
Kim Dae-jung announces "Sunshine Policy" for reconciliation with DPRK

145

CHRONOLOGY & TIMELINE

1987	North Korean agents plant bomb that destroys Korean Airlines Flight 858; massive popular demonstrations for democracy in South Korea.
1990	Soviet Union establishes diplomatic relations with the ROK; series of three meetings between the prime ministers of the two Koreas.
1991	Prime ministers from the two Koreas sign Agreement on Reconciliation, Nonaggression, Exchange, and Cooperation.
1992	People's Republic of China establishes diplomatic relations with the ROK.
1993	Beginning of the North Korean nuclear crisis.
1994	Agreed Framework provides for North Korea to halt its nuclear weapons program in return for funding two light-water nuclear reactors; death of Kim Il Sung.
1996	Financial crisis in East Asia rocks the ROK's economy.
1997	Former dissident Kim Dae-jung elected president of the ROK.
1998	Kim Dae-jung announces "Sunshine Policy" for reconciliation with DPRK.
2000	First meeting of the presidents of the ROK and DPRK in Pyongyang.
2002	Renewal of the North Korean nuclear crisis.
2003	Nullification of the Agreed Framework.
2004	Second session of Six-Party Talks in Beijing fail to resolve the North Korean nuclear dispute with the United States.

NOTES

Chapter 1

1. Bruce Cumings, *The Origins of the Korean War, Vol. II: The Roaring of the Cataract*. Princeton, NJ: Princeton University Press, 1990, p. 619.
2. Gregory Henderson, *Korea: The Politics of the Vortex*. Cambridge, MA: Harvard University Press, 1968, pp. 75, 419n.
3. Soon Sung Cho, *Korea in World Politics, 1941–1950: A Study of American Responsibility*. Berkeley, CA: University of California Press, 1967, p. 196.
4. Ibid., pp. 196–197.
5. Quoted in George M. McCune and Arthur L. Grey, Jr., *Korea Today*. Cambridge, MA: Harvard University Press, 1950, pp. 226–227n.
6. Cho, p. 197.
7. John Merrill, *Korea: The Peninsular Origins of the War*. Newark, DE: University of Delaware Press, 1989, p. 71.
8. James I. Matray, *The Reluctant Crusade: American Foreign Policy in Korea, 1941–1950*. Honolulu: University of Hawaii Press, 1985, p. 147.
9. Cho, pp. 198–199.
10. Merrill, p. 73.
11. Quoted in ibid.
12. Cho, p. 199.
13. Merrill, pp. 73–74.
14. Merrill, pp. 75–76.
15. Cho, p.201.
16. Ibid., p. 76.
17. Matray, pp. 148, 156.
18. Cho, p. 202.
19. McCune and Grey, p. 264.

Chapter 2

20. James Hoare and Susan Pares, *Korea: An Introduction*. London: Kegal Paul International, 1988, pp. 7–13.
21. Takashi Hatada, *A History of Korea*. Santa Barbara, CA: ABC-CLIO, 1969, pp. 1–2.
22. Donald S. Macdonald, *The Koreans: Contemporary Politics and Society*. Boulder, CO: Westview Press, 1990, pp. 9, 26–27.
23. Hoare and Pares, pp. 22–23.
24. John K. Fairbank, Edwin O. Reischauer, and Albert M. Craig, *East Asia: Tradition and Transformation*. Boston: Houghton-Mifflin, 1978, pp. 278–279.
25. Hatada, pp. 8–13, 16–18.
26. Ibid., pp. 18–20.
27. Ibid., pp. 20–23.
28. Keith Pratt and Richard Rutt, *Korea: A Historical and Cultural Dictionary*. Surrey, UK: Curzon Press, 1999, pp. 226, 228, 330–331, 418.
29. Hoare and Pares, pp. 24–25.
30. Fairbank, Reischauer, and Craig, pp. 281–283.
31. Ibid., pp. 284–287.
32. Hatada, pp. 34–52.
33. Fairbank, Reischauer, and Craig, pp. 297–299.
34. Macdonald, pp. 31–32.
35. Fairbank, Reischauer, and Craig, pp. 312–317.
36. Hatada, pp. 79–84.

Chapter 3

37. Fairbank, Reischauer, and Craig, p. 597.
38. Fairbank, Reishauer, and Craig, p. 613.
39. John Wilz, "Encountering Korea: American Perceptions and Policies to 25 June 1950," in *A Revolutionary War: Korea and the Transformation of the Postwar World*, ed. William J. Williams. Chicago: Imprint Publications, 1993, pp. 14–15.
40. Fairbank, Reischauer, and Craig, pp. 319–320, 610.
41. Ibid., pp. 318–323.
42. Hoare and Pares, pp. 40–41.
43. Frederick C. Drake, *The Empire of the Seas: A Biography of Rear Admiral Robert Wilson Shufeldt, USN*. Honolulu: University of Hawaii Press, 1984, pp. 106–107.
44. Wilz, p. 20.
45. Wilz, pp. 20–21.
46. Wilz, p. 21.
47. Ibid.; Hatada, p. 92.
48. Drake, pp. 96–108.
49. Macdonald, pp. 37–38.
50. Hatada, pp. 104–107.
51. Fairbank, Reischauer, and Craig, pp. 625–629.
52. Hoare and Pares, p. 48.

NOTES

53. Fairbank, Reischauer, and Craig, pp. 554–556.

Chapter 4

54. Fairbank, Reischauer, and Craig, pp. 617–618.
55. Wilz, pp. 25, 27–28, 30
56. Quoted in ibid., 26, 28–29.
57. Hoare and Pares, pp. 51–53.
58. Hatada, pp. 113–116.
59. Macdonald, pp. 40–44.
60. Joungwon Kim, *Divided Korea: The Politics of Development*. Cambridge, MA: Harvard University Press, 1976, pp. 39–40, 44.
61. Hatada, pp. 116–122.
62. Hoare and Pares, pp. 58–60.
63. Hatada, pp. 122–126.
64. James I. Matray, *Historical Dictionary of the Korean War*. Westport, CT: Greenwood Press, 1991, pp. 73–74.
65. Matray, *The Reluctant Crusade*, pp. 20–21.
66. Wilz, pp. 36–39, 41–42.
67. Matray, *The Reluctant Crusade*, pp. 31–46.
68. Matray, *Historical Dictionary of the Korean War*, pp. 453–454.

Chapter 5

69. Callum MacDonald, *Korea: The War Before Vietnam*. New York: Free Press, 1986, p. 15.
70. Bruce Cumings, *The Origins of the Korean War, Vol. I: Liberation and the Creation of Separate Regimes, 1945–1947*. Princeton, NJ: Princeton University Press, 1981, pp. 82–89, 139–142.
71. Matray, *The Reluctant Crusade*, pp. 58–64.
72. James I. Matray, ed., *East Asia and the United States: An Encyclopedia of Relations Since 1784*. Westport, CT: Greenwood Press, 2002, pp. 406–407.
73. Kim, pp. 60–62.
74. U.S. Department of State, *The Record on Korean Unification, 1943–1960: Narrative Summary with Principal Documents*. Washington, DC: U.S. Government Printing Office, October 1960, pp. 5–6.
75. McCune and Grey, p. 62.
76. James I. Matray, "Civil War of a Sort: The International Origins of the Korean Conflict," in *Korea and the Cold War: Division, Destruction, and Disarmament*, eds. Kim Chull Baum and James I. Matray. Claremont, CA: Regina Books, 1993, pp. 50–52.
77. Cumings, *The Origins of the Korean War, Vol. I*, pp. 404–427.
78. McCune and Grey, pp. 173–174.
79. Matray, *The Reluctant Crusade*, pp. 110–116, 123–135.
80. Matray, "Civil War of a Sort," pp. 55–57.
81. Matray, *The Reluctant Crusade*, pp. 140–147.
82. McCune and Grey, pp. 226–231.
83. Macdonald, *The Koreans*, pp. 48–49.
84. Quoted in Matray, *The Reluctant Crusade*, p. 165.

Chapter 6

85. Quoted in Burton I. Kaufman, *The Korean War*. Westport, CT: Greenwood Press, 1999, p. 132.
86. Harry S. Truman, *Memoirs, Vol. II: Years of Trial and Hope*. New York: Doubleday, 1956, p. 464.
87. Matray, *Historical Dictionary of the Korean War*, pp. 198–199, 510–511.
88. Matray, *The Reluctant Crusade*, pp. 153–154, 168–170.
89. Ibid., pp. 184–185.
90. James I. Matray, "Dean Acheson's Press Club Speech Reexamined," *Journal of Conflict Studies*, XX, 1 (Spring 2002): 36–37.
91. Ibid., pp. 37–38.
92. Matray, *The Reluctant Crusade*, pp. 197–198, 204–205, 207.
93. Matray, "Dean Acheson's Press Club Speech Reexamined," pp. 38–39.
94. Merrill, pp. 130–140.
95. Ibid., pp. 142–144.
96. Matray, "Dean Acheson's Press Club Speech Reexamined," *Journal of Conflict Studies*, XX, 1 (Spring 2002): p. 43.
97. Ibid., p. 46.
98. Sergei N. Goncharov, John Lewis, and Xue Litai, *Uncertain Partners: Stalin, Mao, and*

NOTES

  the Korean War. Stanford, CA: Stanford University Press, 1993, pp. 136-146.
99. Merrill, pp. 172–177.
100. Kaufman, pp. 7–8.
101. Matray, *Historical Dictionary of the Korean War*, pp. 343-343.
102. Cumings, *The Origins of the Korean War*, Vol. II, pp. 66–85.
103. Jon Halliday and Bruce Cumings, *Korea: The Unknown War.* New York: Pantheon, 1988, pp. 92–103.
104. Matray, *Historical Dictionary of the Korean War*, pp. 341–342.
105. Matray, *Historical Dictionary of the Korean War*, pp. 340–342.
106. Quoted in Joseph C. Goulden, *Korea: The Untold Story of the War.* New York: McGraw-Hill, 1982, p. 3.

Chapter 7

107. Quoted in David Rees. *Korea: The Limited War.* New York: St. Martin's Press, 1964, p. 101.
108. Goncharov, Lewis, and Xue, pp. 174–184.
109. Matray, *Historical Dictionary of the Korean War*, pp. 269–270, 343, 469.
110. Quoted in Goulden, p. 450.
111. Matray, *Historical Dictionary of the Korean War*, pp. 197–198.
112. Matray, *Historical Dictionary of the Korean War*, pp. 197–198, 428–429.
113. Quoted in Kathryn Weathersby, "New Russian Documents on the Korean War," *Cold War International History Project Bulletin*, 6–7: The Cold War in Asia, Winter 1995/1996, pp. 61–62.
114. William Stueck, *The Korean War: An International History.* Princeton, NJ: Princeton University Press, 1994, pp. 209–210.
115. Rosemary Foot, *Substitute for Victory: The Politics of Peacemaking at the Korean Armistice Talks.* Ithaca, NY: Cornell University Press, 1992, pp. 43–44.
116. James F. Schnabel and Robert J. Watson, *History of the Joint Chiefs of Staff: The Joint Chiefs of Staff and National Policy, 1951–1953, Vol. III: The Korean War.* Washington, DC: U.S. Government Printing Office, 1988, pp. 582–587.
117. James I. Matray, "The Korean War," in *Safeguarding the Republic: Essays and Documents in American Foreign Relations, 1890–1991*, Howard Jones. Ed. New York: McGraw Hill, 1992, p. 190.
118. Ibid., pp. 594–595.
119. Walter G. Hermes, *Truce Tent and Fighting Front.* Washington, DC: U.S. Government Printing Office, 1966, pp. 40–44.
120. Matray, *East Asia and the United States*, pp. 461–463.
121. Stueck, pp. 236–237.
122. Quoted in Weathersby, pp. 72–73.
123. Hermes, pp. 114–119.
124. Matray, *East Asia and the United States*, pp. 323–324.
125. Foot, pp. 130–189.

Chapter 8

126. Both quoted in James I. Matray, *The Reluctant Crusade*, pp. 232, 233.
127. Matray, *Historical Dictionary of the Korean War*, pp. 147–148, 400–401, 409–410, 428–429, 511–512.
128. Sidney D. Bailey, *The Korean Armistice.* New York: St. Martin's Press, 1992, pp. 150–170.
129. B.C. Koh, "The War's Impact on the Korean Peninsula," in *A Revolutionary War: Korea and the Transformation of the Postwar World*, ed. William J. Williams. Chicago: Imprint Publications, 1993, pp. 245–246, 253.
130. Matray, *Historical Dictionary of the Korean War*, p. 497.
131. Macdonald, *The Koreans*, pp. 195–196.
132. Kim, pp. 132–162.
133. Matray, *Historical Dictionary of the Korean War*, pp. 355–356.
134. Koh, p. 251.
135. Hoare and Pares, pp. 76–78.
136. Bruce Cumings, *Korea's Place in the Sun: A Modern History.* New York: W.W. Norton, 1997, pp. 346–348.
137. Macdonald, *The Koreans*, pp. 54–55, 197–199.
138. Don Oberdorfer, *The Two Koreas: A Contemporary History.* Reading, PA: Basic

NOTES

Books, 1997, pp. 41–46, 84–115.
139. Hoare and Pares, pp. 182–185.
140. MacDonald, *The Koreans*, pp. 58–59.
141. Matray, *East Asia and the United States*, pp. 569–570.
142. Oberdorfer, pp. 172–178, 186–192.
143. Quoted in James I. Matray, "Korea's Quest for Disarmament and Reunification," in *Korea and the Cold War: Division, Destruction, and Disarmament*, eds. Kim Chull Baum and James I. Matray. Claremont, CA: Regina Books, 1993, p. 242.

Chapter 9

144. Macdonald, *The Koreans*, pp. 44–45.
145. Kim, pp. 182–183.
146. Hoare and Pares, pp. 214–216.
147. Kim, pp. 44–45, 186–187.
148. Koh, p. 248.
149. Dae-sook Suh, *Kim Il Sung: The North Korean Leader*. New York: Columbia University Press, 1988, pp. 141–157.
150. Koh, p. 249.
151. Koh, pp. 248–249.
152. Suh, pp. 269–276.
153. Koh, p. 250.
154. Quoted in ibid., p. 251.
155. Oberdorfer, pp. 19–22.
156. Koh, p. 255.
157. Mitchell B. Lerner, *The Pueblo Incident: A Spy Ship and the Failure of American Foreign Policy*. Lawrence, KS: University Press of Kansas, 2002, pp. 103–116, 213, 222.
158. Macdonald, *The Koreans*, pp. 261–264.
159. Hoare and Pares, pp. 181–182.
160. Oberdorfer, pp. 139–160, 179–196, 229–248.
161. Matray, "Korea's Quest for Disarmament and Reunification," p. 240.
162. Matray, "Korea's Quest for Disarmament and Reunification, " p. 241.
163. Ibid., pp. 240–242.
164. Halliday and Cumings, p. 215.

Chapter 10

165. Koh, pp. 245–246.
166. Matray, "Korea's Quest for Disarmament and Reunification," pp. 242–243.
167. Ibid., pp. 243.
168. Matray, *East Asia and the United States*, pp. 194–195.
169. Oberdorfer, pp. 197–228, 239–248.
170. Matray, "Korea's Quest for Disarmament and Reunification," pp. 245–246.
171. Oberdorfer, pp. 249–259, 265–268.
172. Ibid., pp. 259–265.
173. Matray, "Korea's Quest for Disarmament and Reunification," pp. 248–249.
174. Ibid., pp. 249–250.
175. Matray, "Korea's Quest for Disarmament and Reunification," pp. 252.
176. Ibid., pp. 251–252.
177. Cumings, *Korea's Place in the Sun*, pp. 483–487.
178. Matray, *East Asia and the United States*, pp. 438–439.
179. James I. Matray, "Someplace Else: The Tragedy of Korean-American Relations," *Diplomatic History*, 28, 1 (January 2004), pp. 159–160.
180. Quoted in ibid., p. 159.
181. James I. Matray, "Why South Koreans Think of the United States as a Global Bully," *History News Network* (1 March 2004), <hnn.us/articles/3740.html>.

BIBLIOGRAPHY

Bailey, Sidney D. *The Korean Armistice.* New York: St. Martin's Press, 1992.

Chen, Jian. *China's Road to the Korean War: The Making of the Sino-American Confrontation.* New York: Columbia University Press, 1994.

Cho, Soon Sung. *Korea in World Politics, 1940–1950: An Evaluation of American Responsibility.* Berkeley, CA: University of California Press, 1957.

Conroy, Hilary. *The Japanese Seizure of Korea, 1868–1910: A Study of Realism and Idealism in International Relations.* Philadelphia: University of Pennsylvania Press, 1960.

Cumings, Bruce. *Korea's Place in the Sun: A Modern History.* New York: W.W. Norton, 1997.

――― *The Origins of the Korean War.* Princeton, NJ: Princeton University Press, 1981, 1990.

Drake, Frederick C. *The Empire of the Seas: A Biography of Rear Admiral Robert Wilson Shufeldt, USN.* Honolulu: University of Hawaii Press, 1984.

Fairbank, John K., Edwin O. Reischauer, and Albert M. Craig. *East Asia: Tradition and Transformation.* Boston: Houghton-Mifflin, 1978.

Foot, Rosemary. *Substitute for Victory: The Politics of Peacemaking at the Korean Armistice Talks.* Ithaca, NY: Cornell University Press, 1990.

――― *The Wrong War: American Policy and the Dimensions of the Korean Conflict, 1950–1953.* Ithaca, NY: Cornell University Press, 1985.

Goncharov, Sergei N., John Lewis, and Xue Litai. *Uncertain Partners: Stalin, Mao, and the Korean War.* Stanford, CA: Stanford University Press, 1993.

Goulden, Joseph C. *Korea: The Untold Story of the War.* New York: McGraw-Hill, 1982.

Halliday, Jon and Bruce Cumings. *Korea: The Unknown War.* New York: Pantheon, 1988.

BIBLIOGRAPHY

Han, Sung-ju. *The Failure of Democracy in South Korea.* Berkeley, CA: University of California Press, 1974.

Harrington, Fred Harvey. *God, Mammon and the Japanese: Dr. Horace N. Allen and Korean-American Relations, 1884–1905.* Madison: University of Wisconsin Press, 1944.

Hastings, Max. *The Korean War.* New York: Simon and Schuster, 1987.

Hatada, Takashi. *A History of Korea.* Santa Barbara, CA: ABC-CLIO, 1969.

Henderson, Gregory. *Korea: The Politics of the Vortex.* Cambridge, MA: Harvard University Press, 1968.

Hermes, Walter G. *Truce Tent and Fighting Front.* Washington, DC: U.S. Government Printing Office, 1966.

Hoare, James and Susan Pares. *Korea: An Introduction.* London: Kegal Paul International, 1988.

Kaufman, Burton I. *The Korean War.* Westport, CT: Greenwood Press, 1999.

Kim, Chull Baum and James I. Matray, eds. *Korea and the Cold War: Division, Destruction, and Disarmament.* Claremont, CA: Regina Press, 1993.

Kim, Joungwon. *Divided Korea: The Politics of Development.* Cambridge, MA: Harvard University Press, 1976.

Kim, Se-jin. *The Politics of Military Revolution in Korea.* Chapel Hill, NC: University of North Carolina Press, 1971.

Lee, Yur-bok. *Diplomatic Relations Between the United States and Korea, 1866–1887.* New York: Humanities Press, 1970.

Lerner, Mitchell B. *The Pueblo Incident: A Spy Ship and the Failure of American Foreign Policy.* Lawrence, KS: University Press of Kansas, 2002.

Lowe, Peter. *The Origins of the Korean War.* New York: Longman, 1986.

Macdonald, Donald S. *The Koreans: Contemporary Politics and Society.* Boulder, CO, Westview Press, 1988.

MacDonald, Callum A. *Korea: The War Before Vietnam.* New York: Free Press, 1986.

McCune, George M., and Arthur L. Grey, Jr. *Korea Today.* Cambridge, MA: Harvard University Press, 1950.

Matray, James I. "Dean Acheson's Press Club Speech Reexamined." *Journal of Conflict Studies,* XX, 1 (Spring), 2002.

——— *East Asia and the United States: An Encyclopedia of Relations Since 1784.* Westport, CT: Greenwood Press, 2002, pp. 28–55.

——— *Historical Dictionary of the Korean War.* Westport, CT: Greenwood Press, 1991.

——— *The Reluctant Crusade: American Foreign Policy in Korea, 1941–1950.* Honolulu: University of Hawaii Press, 1985.

——— "Someplace Else: The Tragedy of Korean-American Relations." *Diplomatic History,* 28, 1 (January), 2004, pp. 159–163.

——— "Why South Koreans Think of the United States as a Global Bully." *History News Network,* March 1, 2004, <hnn.us/articles/3740.html>.

Merrill, John. *Korea: The Peninsular Origins of the War.* Newark, DE: University of Delaware Press, 1989.

Nahm, Andrew. *Korea: Tradition and Transformation: A History of the Korean People.* Elizabeth, NJ: Hollym International, 1988.

Oberdorfer, Don. *The Two Koreas: A Contemporary History.* Reading, PA: Basic Books, 1997.

Pratt, Keith, and Richard Rutt, *Korea: A Historical and Cultural Dictionary.* Surrey, UK: Curzon Press, 1999.

Rees, David. *Korea: The Limited War.* New York: St. Martin's Press, 1964.

Schnabel, James F., and Robert J. Watson. *History of the Joint Chiefs of Staff: The Joint Chiefs of Staff and National Policy, 1951–1953, Vol. III: The Korean War.* Washington D.C.: U.S. Government Printing Office, 1988.

Suh, Dae-sook. *Kim Il Sung: The North Korean Leader.* New York: Columbia University Press, 1988.

Stueck, William W. *The Korean War: An International History.* Princeton, NJ: Princeton University Press, 1995.

Truman, Harry S. *Memoirs, Vol. II: Years of Trial and Hope.* New York: Doubleday, 1956.

Weathersby, Kathryn. "New Russian Documents on the Korean War." *Cold War International History Project Bulletin, 6–7: The Cold War in Asia.* Winter 1995/1996, pp. 30–122.

Williams, William J., ed. *A Revolutionary War: Korea and the Transformation of the Postwar World.* Chicago: Imprint Publications, 1993.

INDEX

Acheson, Dean, 86
Age of Imperialism, 31–32, 36
Agreed Framework, 136–38
   nullification, 146
Albright, Madeleine, 138
Allen, Horace N., 37
An Chung-gun, 47
Anglo-Japanese Alliance (1902), 46
Anti-Ballistic Missile Treaty, 139
Anti-Trusteeship Committee, 60, 62
Aritomo Yamagata, 40
Armistice
   and the Korean War, 2, 14, 83, 87, 89–92, 96–99, 102–4, 115, 119–21, 133, 143
Arthur, Chester A., 39
Austin, Warren R., 5

Beijing, 32, 37–38, 79, 125, 146
   and the DPRK, 86–87, 90–91, 120–21, 123, 132
   Koguryo forces in, 19
   and the Korean War, 93, 95, 98–99, 121
   and ROK, 113
   and the UN, 104
Bradley, Omar N., 89
Buddhism, 18–19, 21, 25, 28
   state religion, 142
Bush, George H.W., 133, 135
Bush, George W., 139–40
Byrnes, James F., 59–60

Cairo Conference, 52–53
Cairo Declaration, 54, 143–44
Capitalism, 61, 63, 113
Carter, James, 111, 136
Chae-pil (Philip Jaisohn), 40
Chang Myon, 108–9, 111
Changsu, King, 21
Cheju-do Island, 16
Chemulpo, 35, 39
Chemulpo, Treaty of, 37–39, 46, 64, 142
China, 16–17, 48–49, 60
   communism, 75, 80, 90, 98, 104, 118
   culture, 19–21, 32, 64–65, 80–81
   and Korean control, 18, 22–25, 31–35, 37–40, 106, 142
   military, 83, 86–88, 90–91, 98, 101
   philosophy, 21
   politics, 117–18, 121, 123–24
   at war, 28, 52

Chinese People's Volunteers Army, 87, 143
Chingghis Khan, 23–24
Cho Man-sik, 79
chonmin, 26
Cho So-ang, 3–4
Choson Dynasty, 25, 28–29, 47–48, 142
   class system, 26–27
   isolation, 32–36
Christianity, 32–34, 142
Chunchon, 78
Chun Du-hwan, 111–12
chungin, 26
Churchill, Winston, 53–54, 63
Clinton, Bill, 135–36, 138
Cold War
   end of, 2, 130, 140
   international tensions, 3, 84
   and Korea, 58, 63, 67, 69, 129
Committee for the Preparation of Korean Independence, 115
Communism, 68
   and China, 75, 80, 90, 98, 104, 118
   and North Korea, 3, 5, 7–8, 12, 50, 59–60, 66, 70, 72–73, 78–79, 81–83, 86–87, 91–96, 101, 103, 105, 108–9, 116–18, 120–22, 125, 129–31, 136
   and the Soviet Union, 55, 61, 63, 99, 101, 117–18
Confederal Republic of Koryo, 124, 144–45
Confucius
   philosophy, 18–19, 21, 25–27, 33, 142
Council of Foreign Ministers (1945), 59
Cuban Missile Crisis, 122

demilitarized zone. *See* DMZ
Democratic Front for the Unification of the Fatherland. *See* DFUF
Democratic People's Republic of Korea. *See* DPRK
Democratic National Coalition Front, 7
DFUF, 79
DMZ, 16, 77, 123, 125, 132, 134–35
   and the armistice, 86, 92–93, 95–97, 99, 105, 143
   Soviet and American zones, 55–56, 59, 65, 67–68, 115, 140
   tunnels, 124, 145
DPRK, 2, 104, 109–10, 137, *see also* North Korea
   collapse, 121, 127, 140
   constitution, 118

155

INDEX

establishment, 69–70, 143
government, 115–27, 130–40
military, 72–73, 75–83, 86–87, 91, 95, 124
reconciliation, 112–13, 145–46
in the United Nations, 144
Dulles, John Foster, 101–2

Eisenhower, Dwight D., 98, 102–3

First Opium War, 31, 34
Foote, Lucius H., 37, 39
France
in Korea, 32–35, 37, 105

General Sherman (American schooner), 34, 38, 142
Geneva Conference, 64, 98, 103–5, 144–45
Germany
in Korea, 37, 113
reunification, 129–32
Gorbachev, Mikhail, 131
Great Britain
in Korea, 31–32, 37, 41, 46, 52, 63

Hangul, 17, 51, 142
Han River, 17, 19, 21–22
Hideyoshi Toyotomi, 27–28
Hiroshima, 55
Ho Chi Minh, 105
Hodge, John R., 3, 7, 12, 59, 66–67
Hong Myong-hui, 4

IAEA, 133, 135–36
Inchon, 115
Independence Club, 40–41
International Atomic Energy Agency. *See* IAEA
International Monetary Fund, 138
Ito Hirobumi, 47

Jaisohn, Philip. *See* Chae-pil
Japan, 16, 24, 110, 138, 140
control of Korea, 6, 24, 45–55, 64, 129
culture, 19
invasion of Korea, 27–28, 31, 37–43, 117, 142–44

and World War II, 13, 70, 76, 115
Jiang Jieshi, 50, 53–54
Joy, C. Turner, 91, 96–97
Juche, 120–21, 123

Kaesong, 24, 77–79, 91, 93, 95–96, 143
Kanghwa Island, 34–35, 37, 142
Kanghwa, Treaty of, 37, 142
KCIA, 110–11
Kennan, George, 46–47
Kim Chong-won, 83
Kim Dae-jung, 110, 112, 144
president of ROK, 136, 138–39, 146
seizure of, 145
"sunshine policy," 136–38, 145–46
Kim Du-bong, 4, 7, 9, 13, 69
Kim Gu
assassination, 14
and the KPG, 49–50, 54, 60
and the North-South conference, 3–4, 7–10, 12–13, 68
Kim Jong Il,
and DPRK, 77, 120–21, 126–27, 136–38, 141
Kim Il Sung, 50–51
death of, 76–77, 126, 137, 146
and DPRK, 69, 73–75, 78–79, 86–87
goals, 12–13, 82–83, 91, 99, 131, 135, 144–45
leadership, 4, 7, 9, 63–64, 73–75, 101, 115–24
Kim Kyu-sik
leadership, 2–9, 12–14, 49, 66, 68
Kim Song-ju. *See* Kim Il Sung
Kim Song-su, 10
Kim Young-sam, 77, 135
Ko-Choson, 17, 142
fall of, 18–19
Koguryo
collapse, 22–23
culture, 21
formation, 19, 142
military power, 19
Kojong, King, 34, 36, 38–42, 45–46, 64
death, 48
Kongmin, King, 25
Korea, *see also* North Korea; South Korea
annexation of, 143
chronology and timeline, 143–46
creation myth, 17
division, 2, 6 7, 143

INDEX

economy, 27, 33, 64, 66, 103–4, 106–7, 112, 115–16, 121, 131, 138
elections, 3, 7, 10–11, 13, 61, 66–69, 143–44
foreign policy, 31–43, 72–73
founding of, 17, 142
geography, 16–17
independence, 4, 10, 39, 48–51, 53–54, 67, 129, 143–44
language, 17, 51, 142
nickname, 18, 31–33
postwar reconstruction, 45–47, 52–53, 58, 60–62
religions, 17–19, 21, 33–34, 37, 39, 142
reunification attempts, 10, 58, 60–61, 63, 66–67, 75, 77, 79, 82, 84, 99, 101, 104, 109, 111, 113, 116, 127, 129, 132, 138, 140, 144–45
unification, 22, 24, 59, 72, 79, 142, 144
wartime, 35, 58, 72–84, 86–99, 142–44
Korea Democratic Party, 106
Korean Central Intelligence Agency. *See* KCIA
Korean Commission, 64
Korean People's Republic, 58, 65, 143–44
legitimacy, 59
Korean Provisional Government. *See* KPG
Korean Restoration Army, 54
Korean War, 4, 72–99, 105, 107–8, 137
after, 16, 65, 109, 111, 116–17, 119–22, 130, 136, 139
armistice, 2, 14, 83, 87, 89–92, 96–99, 102–4, 115, 119–21, 133, 143
conventional phase, 2, 86
"first," 35
reason, 45, 101, 129, 145
Korean Worker's Party, 4, 116–18
Korea's Supreme People's Assembly, 13
Koryo, 25, 27, 29
establishment, 24, 142
KPA, 74, 78, 81–82, 86, 91
KPG, 143
leaders, 49–50, 54, 64
Kung Ye, 23
Kwangju, 19, 21, 112
incident, 145
Kyongju, 20, 24
Kyon Hwan, 23

League of Nations, 64
Lenin, Vladimir, 50
Li Hongzhang, 37–39
Low, Frederick F., 35

MAC, 96–97
MacArthur, Douglas, 70, 87, 89
MacDonald, Callum, 58
Malik, Jacob A., 90
Manchuria, 21, 40, 42, 45, 50, 52, 54, 87
invasion of Korea, 17, 28, 142
Mao Zedong, 75, 79, 86–88, 90–91, 99, 117, 120
March First Movement, 13, 48–49, 51, 64, 65, 77–78, 116, 143
Marshall, George C., 4
Marshall Plan, 67
Military Armistice Commission. *See* MAC
Miller, Molly, 38
Ming Dynasty, 25, 28
Molotov, Vyacheslav, 59–60
Mongol, 17, 20
invasion of Korea, 23–25, 29, 142
Moscow Agreement on Korea, 60–63, 65, 143
Muccio, John J., 73

Nam Il, 91, 93, 97–98
Nanjing
government of, 50
Nanjing, Treaty of, 31
Neutral Nations Supervisory Commission, 97
Nixon, Richard M., 111
No Mu-hyun, 137, 140
No Tae-u, 112–13, 131, 133, 135
North Korea, 16, 52, 61, 63–64, 98–99, 141, *see also* DPRK
constitution, 7
economy, 116, 121
government, 3, 5, 7–8, 10, 12, 14, 65, 67, 69–70, 79, 109, 115, 118, 120–21, 125–26, 129–31, 136
military, 72, 76–77, 81–82, 97, 101, 103, 123–24
nuclear weapons, 11, 77, 132–40, 146
tunnels, 124, 145
war with South, 2, 72–75, 78, 80–83, 87, 89–91, 93–95, 101, 108, 143–46
North Korean People's Army (KPA), 8
North Korean People's Committee, 4, 13
North-South Conference, 2, 7, 11–13, 68, 143
Nuclear Non-Proliferation Treaty (NPT), 133, 136

Okinawa, 55
Ongjin Peninsula, 77–78

157

INDEX

Open Door Policy, 42–43
Operational Ratkiller, 108
Oriental Development Company, 51
Outlook, The, 46–47

Paekche
    collapse, 22–23
    culture, 21
    formation, 19, 142
Pak Chong-hui, 109–11
    assassination of, 145
    power seize, 144
Pak Hon-yong, 76, 78–79, 117, 120
    assassination, 118
Panmunjom, 95, 97, 102–4
Peng Dehuai, 91
People's Republic of China (PRC)
    and the armistice, 91
    and DPRK, 77
    establishment, 78
    and the Geneva Conference, 104
    and Korea, 79, 86–87, 89, 93, 120, 122–24, 130–32, 140, 146
    and the United States, 98–99, 102, 111
Philippines, 43, 46
Portsmouth, Treaty of, 42, 143–44
Potsdam Conference, 53, 55
PRC. *See* People's Republic of China
Provisional People's Committee, 64, 66
Pusan, 45, 81–82, 101, 117
Pyongyang, 16–17, 93, 140
    Chinese occupation of, 22
    Japanese occupation of, 52
    and Korean War, 74–78, 82–83, 86, 90, 95, 98–99
    military, 116, 119, 133–34, 136
    radio, 7, 12
    reunification meetings in, 2, 8–9, 69, 79, 113, 137–38, 143, 145–46
    self-reliance, 121–27, 131–32

Qing Dynasty, 28, 32, 37

Reconciliation, Nonagression, Exchange, and Cooperation Agreement, 145–46
Republic of Korea. *See* ROK
Ridgway, Matthew B., 87, 89–91, 95
ROK, 2, 6, 13, 101, 138, *see also* South Korea
    constitution, 50
    economy, 105–6, 113, 131, 146
    establishment, 5, 64–65, 69–70, 143–44
    leaders, 72–73, 104, 108–9, 111, 115, 119, 123–27, 130, 133–38, 140
    military, 74–79, 81–83, 87, 89, 45, 102, 110, 112
    relationship with People's Republic of China, 146
    and the UN, 132
Roosevelt, Franklin D., 53–54, 64, 143
Roosevelt, Theodore, 42, 46–47, 64
Root-Takahira Agreement, 38
Russia, 16, 140, 143–44, *see also* Soviet Union
    in Korea, 31–32, 37–38, 40, 48, 50, 59, 62
    at war, 41–42
Russo-Japanese War, 41–42, 45–46, 64, 143

Second Opium War, 31
Sejong, King, 25
Seoul, 6, 19, 25, 60, 69, 110, 136, 140, 144
    demonstrations, 81
    foreign occupations, 28, 32, 36, 39–40, 45, 47, 52, 64
    and Korean War, 14, 82, 101–2
    Olympic games, 112, 124
    reunification meetings in, 7, 12, 50, 62, 79, 123–26, 131–32, 134, **138**
Shtykov, Terenti, 62, 74–75, 78
Shufeldt, Robert W., 37–39
Siberia, 50, 54
Silla, 29
    "bone rank," 20
    collapse, 23–24
    formation, 20, 142, 144
    "head rank," 21
    military, 22
Sino-Japanese War, 40, 142
Sino-Soviet Treaty of Friendship and Alliance, 79
Sinuiju, 45
sirhak, 33
SKIG, 66
SKILA, 2, 8, 13, 65–66
Socialist Democratic Party, 3
Sojong
    development of Hangul, 142
South Korea, 12, 16, 56, 129, *see also* ROK
    capital, 6
    demonstrations, 146
    economy, 131, 138

INDEX

government, 5, 7, 9–10, 13, 67, 70, 104–11, 113, 136–40
military, 83, 98, 102–3, 123, 125–26
and the UN, 132–34
war with North, 2, 5, 72–77, 86–87, 90, 99, 101, 143, 145–46
South Korean Assembly, 101
South Korean Interim Government. See SKIG
South Korean Interim Legislature Assembly. See SKILA
Soviet-American Commission, 4–5, 62–63, 67
withdrawal, 11, 72
Soviet-North Korean Treaty of Friendship and Alliance, 74
Soviet Union, 2, 5, 7
and communism, 55, 61, 63, 99, 101, 117–18
in Korea, 45, 49, 53–55, 59–66, 69, 72, 74–76, 78–79, 87–88, 90–91, 98–99, 105
military, 115–18, 120–23
relationship with DPRK, 9, 11–12, 101, 103–4, 130
relationship with ROK, 131, 146
Stalin, Joseph, 118
and communism, 55, 61, 63, 122
death, 98–99
and Korea, 53–54, 58, 74–76, 78–79, 86, 88, 90–91, 120, 143
"Sunshine Policy," 136–38, 145–46
Supreme Korean People's Assembly, 69, 79
Syngman Rhee (Yi Sung-man), 40–41
and the March First Movement, 13, 49, 78, 111, 116
and the North-South conference, 3, 8, 10
regime, 74, 79, 81–83, 116, 119
and reunification, 90–91, 99, 101–4
and ROK, 13, 50, 54, 64–66, 69, 72–73, 77, 86, 106–9, 144

Taedong River, 17–18, 34, 80
Taejon, 81
Taewongun, "Grand Prince," 34–35, 38
Taft-Katsura Agreement, 38, 46
Taiping Rebellion, 31
Taiwan, 40
Tangun, 17, 142
Thirty-eighth parallel, 24
border clashes, 56, 64, 68–69, 83–84, 101, 139
military occupation at, 2, 55, 58–59, 63, 72, 74, 76, 86–87, 95, 115, 119, 143–44

Three Kingdoms Era, 16, 19–20, 29, 142, 144
Tianjin, Treaty of, 31, 38–39
Tokyo, 37–39, 42, 47, 145
Tonghak Rebellion, 142
Trans-Siberian Railroad, 42
Truman Doctrine, 67
Truman, Harry S., 53–55, 58–59, 63, 66–68, 70, 72–73, 83, 86–88, 94–95, 98, 101
Tsushima Island, 16
Tumen River, 16, 50
Two Brothers (American whaler), 32

UNC, 92–98, 118
United Korean Legislative Organ, 11
United Nations
general assembly, 4–5, 67
ground troops, 88–89, 91, 93, 95, 101, 108
resolutions, 2–4, 10, 61, 67–69, 73, 76, 78–79, 81, 83, 90, 105–6, 143
security council, 5, 132
and South Korea, 125–26, 132–33, 145
United Nations Command. See UNC
United Nations Korean Reconstruction Agency. See UNKRA
United Nations Temporary Commission on Korea. See UNTCOK
United States, 2
in Korea, 32, 35, 37–39, 41–43, 45–46, 49, 52, 54–56, 74, 81, 105, 108
military, 7, 9, 11, 66, 70, 72–73, 77, 79, 83, 86–90, 91, 93, 95–96, 98–99, 101, 115, 117, 119, 123–25, 129–31, 136, 145
nuclear crisis with North Korea, 133–40, 146
occupation zone, 7, 10, 55–56, 58–60, 62–63, 65–66, 68–70
treaties with Korea, 5, 37–39, 42, 102, 112–13
UNKRA, 106
UNTCOK, 2–5, 7–8, 11–12, 67–69
U.S.-ROK Mutual Defense Treaty, 102, 125

Versailles Conference, 48–50
Vietnam, 104–5, 123, 130

Wang Kon, 24
Wei-man, 18
Wilson, Woodrow, 48–50
Wonsan, 16, 32, 91, 93

159

INDEX

World War I, 48
World War II, 2, 4, 6, 13, 45, 49, 52–53, 61, 64, 70, 76, 115, 129
Wu-Ti, 20, 142

Yalu (Amnok) River, 16–19, 22, 24, 50–51, 86, 98
Yalta Conference, 54, 64, 143
yangban, 26, 33
yangmin, 26–27
Yi Dynasty, 25, 28–29
    government, 32–35, 38, 40–41, 47
Yi Song-gye, 25
    and the Choson Dynasty, 142
Yi Sung-man. *See* Syngman Rhee
Yi Sun-sin, 28
Yixin, 39
Yo Un-hong, 3
Yo Un-hyong, 3, 115

Zhou Wen-mu
    execution, 33

PICTURE CREDITS

page:

Maps on pages ii and xiii
    Fairbank, John K., Edwin Reischauer, and Albert Craig, EAST ASIA: TRADITION AND TRANSFORMATION, Revised Edition. © 1989 by Houghton Mifflin Company. Used with permission.

6	© Hulton|Archive, by Getty Images
23	© Hulton|Archive, by Getty Images
36	Library of Congress, LC-USZ62-72797
41	© Hulton|Archive, by Getty Images
53	Courtesy The National Archives
61	Library of Congress
80	Associated Press, AP/Mex Desfor
88	Associated Press, AP
94	Courtesy The National Archives
102	Associated Press, AP
107	© Bettmann/CORBIS
122	© CORBIS
139	Associated Press, AP/David Longstreath

ABOUT THE CONTRIBUTORS

James I. Matray is professor of history and chair at California State University, Chico. He has published more than forty articles and book chapters on U.S.-Korean relations during and after World War II. Author of *The Reluctant Crusade: American Foreign Policy in Korea, 1941–1950* and *Japan's Emergence as a Global Power*, his most recent publication is *East Asia and the United States: An Encyclopedia of Relations Since 1784*. Matray also is international columnist for the *Donga Ilbo* in South Korea.

George J. Mitchell served as chairman of the peace negotiations in Northern Ireland during the 1990s. Under his leadership, an historic accord, ending decades of conflict, was agreed to by the governments of Ireland and the United Kingdom and the political parties in Northern Ireland. In May 1998, the agreement was overwhelmingly endorsed by a referendum of the voters of Ireland, North and South. Senator Mitchell's leadership earned him worldwide praise and a Nobel Peace Prize nomination. He accepted his appointment to the U.S. Senate in 1980. After leaving the Senate, Senator Mitchell joined the Washington, D.C. law firm of Piper Rudnick, where he now practices law. Senator Mitchell's life and career have embodied a deep commitment to public service and he continues to be active in worldwide peace and disarmament efforts.